# The Definitive Guide to Spiritual Warfare

Wake up the mighty men,
sound the alarm,
prepare for war

## ROGER ROBINS

Ark House Press
arkhousepress.com

© 2025 Roger Robins

All rights reserved. Apart from any fair dealing for the purpose of study, research, criticism, or review, as permitted under the Copyright Act, no part may be reproduced by any process without written permission.

Unless otherwise stated, all Scriptures are taken from the New International Translation (Holy Bible. Copyright© 1996, 2004, 2007, 2013 by Tyndale House Foundation. Used by permission of Tyndale House Publishers Inc., Carol Stream, Illinois 60188. All rights reserved.)

Cataloguing in Publication Data:
Title: The Definitive Guide to Spiritual Warfare
ISBN: 978-1-7642308-0-3 (pbk)
Subjects: REL074000 RELIGION / Christian Ministry / Pastoral Resources; REL067060 RELIGION / Christian Theology / Eschatology; REL070000 RELIGION / Christianity / General.

Design by initiateagency.com

*Dedicated to Jesus Christ the author and finisher of my faith*

# Contents

Preface .................................................................................... vii

Part I: A Soul's Journey ............................................................. 1
    Chapter 1: Read Me First ..................................................... 3
    Chapter 2: Journey into Darkness ........................................ 5
    Chapter 3: Journey into Light ............................................. 17

Part II: The Way of the Flesh .................................................. 31
    Chapter 4: Me Myself and I ................................................ 33
    Chapter 5: Spiritual Blindness ............................................ 44
    Chapter 6: Who are you? .................................................... 60
    Chapter 7: Submission ....................................................... 66

Part III: The Way of the World ............................................... 71
    Chapter 8: World Views ..................................................... 73
    Chapter 9: Influence of Media ............................................ 79
    Chapter 10: Influence of Social Media ................................ 83
    Chapter 11: Peer Pressure .................................................. 90
    Chapter 12: Misinformation .............................................. 99
    Chapter 13: Discernment .................................................. 109
    Chapter 14: Being upbeat in a downbeat world ................. 118

Part IV: The Way of the Devil ............................................................... 127
    Chapter 15: Know your enemy ................................................. 129
    Chapter 16: Schemes of the Devil .............................................. 139

Part V: Warfare ........................................................................................ 153
    Chapter 17: The Battle ................................................................ 155
    Chapter 18: Footholds ................................................................ 171
    Chapter 19: Strongholds ............................................................ 186
    Chapter 20: The Church ............................................................. 216
    Chapter 21: Spiritual Protection ................................................ 224
    Chapter 22: Intercession ............................................................. 242
    Chapter 23: Intercession That Backfires ................................... 251
    Chapter 24: Evicting Demonic Squatters ................................. 257

Epilogue .................................................................................................. 263
Notes ....................................................................................................... 267
About the Author ................................................................................. 271

# Preface

It's the year 2024, and my wife has been invited to her nephew's wedding at a grand old manor house beside the river in Edinburgh, Scotland. I could see she was eager to go, and I viewed it as an opportunity to take a break from work. We decided to enhance the trip by spending a week in the Outer Hebrides, Isle of Lewis. My wife wanted to see the birthplace of the revival that took place there about seventy years ago.

We based ourselves in the town of Stornoway and planned to make day trips from there. By chance, there was a Christian revival conference that same week, in Stornoway, in an old church called Martin's Memorial Church.

> *Man makes his plans, but God establishes them.*
> (Prov 16:9)

While on the flight from Sydney to Edinburgh, I happened to be listening to an audio teaching from Chuck Missler. Probably one of the greatest Bible teachings of the 20$^{th}$ and 21$^{st}$ centuries. I was listening to his teaching on Revelation chapter six, The White Horse, The Red Horse, The Black Horse & the Pale Horse. I am not normally drawn to prophetic teaching. But these four horses bring war, famine, and pestilence. With the Pale Horse comes the death of a quarter of the earth's population. Chuck's conclusion is that this is only possible with a nuclear exchange. I was one hundred percent convinced this would not happen in my lifetime. But one hundred percent convinced it would happen in my children's lifetime. I suddenly had an enormous burden for this up-and-coming generation who are oblivious to the terrible days ahead. This would set the stage for what was to follow.

It was Saturday morning of the conference, and the pastor's wife, Donna MacNeil, got up to speak on spiritual warfare. She wasn't a big lady, nor did she appear threatening in any way. But what she had to say would shake me to my core. She wasn't teaching anything I didn't already know, yet I found myself having to learn it all over again. Where have I been for the last forty years? How is it that I need to learn this all over again? So, I began to weep.

The moment pastor Donna finished I ran up to her to ask if she'd consider holding a Spiritual Warfare conference and expounding further on the material she had just covered. Her face went blank, and she did not say a word. Just as I said to myself, "You've done all you can," the Holy Spirit spoke to me in a small, still voice, "You could write a book".

No, I've entertained vain thoughts like that before. I'm not going to deceive myself yet again. So, I said to the Holy Spirit, "If this is of you and not me, let me float the idea by my wife. If she tells me I have delusions of grandeur, then I'll know it was me. If she turns and is supportive, then it's of you." My wife has proven to be more in tune with God and is quick to humble me.

To my surprise, my wife was supportive. No sooner had she finished encouraging me than the Holy Spirit began to reveal the structure of the book and the subject matter I needed to cover. The introduction would discuss how I came to Christ and everything that happened afterwards, as many of the challenges contained lessons that this generation needs to know. In that revelation, I understood that everything I had lived through was climaxing at this moment in time.

The purpose of this book is to help prepare this generation for the troubled times ahead. So you can be all that Christ has called you to be.

# PART I
# A Soul's Journey

Prov 4:25 Let your eyes look straight ahead, and your eyelids look right before you. Ponder the path of your feet.

# Read Me First

Everytime you read a book (like this), hear a presentation, or complete a training course, most people will forget up to eighty percent of the content in the first twenty-four hours. Then, if the instruction requires you to make lifestyle changes, only ten percent of those who remember anything will make that change.

Most Sundays, you have a pastor teaching the word of God, with instructions on how to live a Godly life. Do you remember what he taught last week? Did you apply those lifestyle changes? Guess what. There's nothing wrong with the pastor.

By reflecting on what was taught one hour after the presentation and then again, the next day, you won't forget anything. You can be the ten percent guy. [1]

## About This Book

I want to make it perfectly clear that this is not a book on how to kick demons out of people. Although deliverance is one aspect of spiritual warfare, it is not an end in itself. This book has a strong psychological flavour to it, as the battlefield is in the mind. As you think, so you become.

The book is divided into five sections:

1. A Soul's Journey
2. The Way of the Flesh
3. The Way of the World
4. The Way of the Devil
5. Warfare

It is best read sequentially instead of jumping to chapters you think you need to know. The biggest blocker in learning anything new is thinking you already know it.

It is my desire that this book will help prepare you for the dark days that are coming as part of the end times. As darkness increases, light must shine even brighter.

Remember, this is your time on the earth. A time to not just impact history but impact eternity. You and God are a majority every day of the week. You are more than a conqueror through Christ, who strengthens YOU.

# Journey into Darkness

The story that follows contains a secret to a secret. It is my desire that you know and understand the secret.

I realised once I left school that the thugs were the ones studying martial art and boxing. Not those who needed those skills. So, I went looking for a martial arts system that would train a man for all seasons. (All situations)

I found what I was looking for at a school called Togakure Ryu. This institution offers a diverse range of areas of study that extend beyond unarmed combat. It teaches a commando-style fighting system infused with mystical elements, attracting a considerable number of military personnel and veterans.

In my second year of training, I met a karate instructor who held a 4th Dan black belt. To this day, he is one of the fastest men I have ever known. In the time it takes you to blink, he could strike you three times. Often, when I was alone with him, he would speak of the forbidden training he used to do and the strange experiences he had. So, I took him out, got him drunk, and so learned his secrets.

For the first three months of forbidden training, a type of eastern meditation, I experienced a sense of peace and happiness unlike anything I had felt before. The more I trained, the better it became. It was akin to being high on drugs. After three months, I reached a mental state similar to an LSD trip and started to hallucinate.

I approached a friend of mine, an ex-kung fu master named Rodney. He was a man of great knowledge but not of great skill. This was primarily due to his habit of importing books for customers from around the world; during the weekdays, he would read his customers' books and then sell them to them on weekends. He did this to me numerous times. As a result, he gained great knowledge.

Rodney had advanced as far as possible in Wing Chun kung fu without being Chinese. He had delved into internal training and had combined it with LSD, which ultimately led to him spending twelve months with a psychiatrist.

He explained that in the higher realms of martial arts, there are internal martial arts such as Tai Chi and Qigong. In the higher realms of Tai Chi, there is yoga, not just simple stretching, but complex breathing exercises. Both yoga and martial arts use the same psychic force. In Martial Arts, it's called Chi, and in Yoga, it's called Kundalini. Martial Artists use it to develop great physical abilities, and yogis use it to develop great psychic abilities.

Knowing this, I brought a book on yoga. Not just any book, but a secret manuscript called "The Serpent Fire". However, the book was written back to front, with the beginner's exercises in the back and the advanced exercises in the front. This was done so that the uninitiated like myself would become very sick and die.

By some miracle of God, I only did the first exercise for five minutes, and suddenly, my body began to shake violently as my spirit started to rise upwards. Terror filled me as I thought I was dying. This was my first out-of-the-body experience. So, I ran outside, and somehow, the fresh air settled me. Half an hour later, I was driving down the road when it started again. While driving down the road, my spirit uncontrollably began to lift up and out of my body. I then realised I'd begun something that was uncontrollable and terrifying.

Vanity began to enter the picture as I became convinced I'd experienced and overcome death, and, in fact, that I was invincible. I kept training, and the psychic experiences increased in ferocity. Once, while walking down York Street in Sydney, my body suddenly stood still, and I went forward, and a kaleidoscope of colours passed by me. These experiences also followed me into my sleep. I remember sitting up in bed only to find I was still lying down. One night, when this happened, something attacked me, and after that, I was too scared to go to sleep.

I went back to the kung fu master and the karateka to tell them what had happened to me. Both of them warned me, "You must stop training, or you will die". For the first time in my life, I felt some peace and happiness, yet these guys tell me I'm dying. After all, the exercises that I was doing were just breathing exercises. You have to breathe to live, right?

They explained, "The energy force travels from the base of the spine up through seven psychic centres to the brain, where it biologically alters the brain structure, opening up the brain for telepathy and clairvoyance. If the energy force is misdirected, it destroys the brain structure, causing loss of function of bodily organs, various types of insanity, and death. This is what very likely killed Bruce Lee.

Now, at last, I understood why it was called forbidden training. This energy force is the underlying mechanism behind most self-development systems and all psychic phenomena outside of the church. **This is the secret of Yoga and Martial Arts.**

Still, I did not listen; I was convinced I would succeed where they had failed. I had a strong spirit and a strong mind. I had overcome death. Nothing could stop me, nothing. At this point, I should have died. For I did not listen but kept training.

God gave me a dream; someone poured petrol over me and set me alight. I screamed for help, but no one came; I rolled on the ground, yet the flames continued to burn. I was dying. When I woke, I understood the dream. The fire represented the Serpent Fire or Chi, and calling out with no reply indicated that there was no one who could assist me. This time I listened, for the knowledge came from within and not from the mouth of a man. I dreamed again; I was walking up a mountain with a blindfold on. Suddenly, the blindfold was removed. I was on the edge of a great precipice, and one more step and I'd be over the edge. This dream speaks for itself.

By now, I was convinced that the chi was killing me, yet I felt compelled to continue the internal training, as if the chi had an intelligence of its own and wanted to kill me. One other question that stuck in the back of my mind was whether my sanity was intact. Even though I had knowledge of psychology, I could not be sure. I had definitely changed.

I stopped all meditation and continued only with physical training. Some time passed, and a friend told me about a book called "Death of a Guru" written by the son of the Greatest Guru ever to come out of India. (Maharaj 1984)[2] This seemed to be the missing piece to my jigsaw. The book explained how chi was a demonic energy force creating a demonic oppression in the students, and by the time it reaches the brain, it becomes demonic possession. Then I remembered how I thought the chi had an intelligence of its own. It really did. **This is the Secret to the Secret; the energy force isn't an energy force, it's an entity.**

I went back to my book, The Serpent Fire, and read the introduction, which I had skipped the first time; it read, "Yoga is the Highest Secret of all Occult Doctrines". I had great trouble dealing with this reality. It wasn't what I wanted to believe. Then I remembered my Mikkyo (a combination of Buddhism and Tantric Yoga) teachings: "Be there", "Keep your mind where your body is", and "Insist on reality". But what was reality?

I had heard that rebirthing could help people affected by chi training, so I decided to visit a practitioner. I was placed in a trance through connected breathing and experienced severe cramping in my hands and legs. This was both torturous and terrifying. The breathing felt suspicious to me. A bit of research revealed that re-birthing was introduced to Western society by a man named Leonard Ore, who was a student of a man called Babba Ji, a powerful yogi who practised and taught kundalini yoga, the very sickness I was trying to escape. This was yet another trap in the journey through life.

Next, I went to a therapist to see if my sanity was intact. For forty dollars a session, he introduced me to exercises called "The Feldenkrais Method". He didn't tell me if I was crazy, or he would lose his forty dollars a week. Now, it was my final year of training, and I was only engaged in physical training; yet I could feel the chi growing rather than diminishing. I bought a book called "Occult Shock and Psychic Forces."[3] It described Feldenkrais as a form of occultism based on yoga. Yet another trap in the journey through life.

If I'm possessed, maybe I can get exorcised. I remembered a doctor I once visited who was both a Christian and knowledgeable about spiritual matters. If anyone could tell me whether I was possessed, it would be him. So, I went to his surgery and had a chat. He assured me that if I was able to come to his surgery and discuss the possibility of demon possession, it was unlikely that I was truly possessed, as possessed people are not in control of themselves. However, because I had been open to occultism, I was, in fact, demon-possessed, and I could expect reoccurrences of psychic experiences for as long as the oppression existed. My only chance was to turn to God.

I walked away from the surgery that day, believing it was all a bad dream, and I could not comprehend this reality. My training had been the solution to all my problems, and now it was the problem.

Having gone into denial about everything that had happened, I decided to train with my teacher one last time before retiring. You see, my teacher lived on the other side of the planet, in a place called Dayton in central Ohio. I travelled there once a year to train. I believed in an ultimate fighting system that could produce a man for all seasons or all situations. While training saved me from the problems of life, what was going to save me from training?

One of the closely guarded secrets of the Togakure Ryu was the secret of "Kuji In" finger weaving, combined with controlled breathing. Once back in the States, I got my teacher Steve alone and laid it on him. "What is Kuji In"? What is it really? He answered, "What does it matter if you're summoning demons to do your bidding so long as your objectives are achieved". I couldn't believe what I heard, and I didn't ask any more questions. Nor did I ever speak with him again.

In the dojo (training hall) the next day, I met a guy called David Cozz, a Delta Force Commando who had been raised by an Indian mystic, and he was teaching the class. He was a man of great skill. He had the class sit down in a circle, gave one guy a knife to attack him with, and proceeded to throw his attacker without physically touching him. He moved to one side, and as he rotated his hands, his adversary did a somersault and landed on his back. Later, I asked him what the minimum time it would take to learn to do this. He said, "One week." I replied, "But surely it would take longer to train the mind." He told me, "The mind had nothing to do with it; it was all in the spirit. A person's upbringing and their own attitudes cause them to put limitations on themselves, restricting them from any great achievements." Then, I understood how weakness in character creates limiting factors.

One last thing he told me. "The real fight was behind the scenes in the spiritual realm." As he said this, a vision came into my mind. I saw a theatre and actors on a stage. Most people only got to see what was happening on the stage; only a few got to look behind the scenes, behind the stage. He added, "That is why it is not always right to meet hostility with hostility. If you treat hostility with kindness, then you defuse the hostility and break the demonic powers from behind the scenes. (The truth is that God sets the stage each day. All the props belong to Him.)

I was such a closed book that God was using unchurched people to speak to me.

Mikkyo Teachings taught me to view things from the scheme of totality, or like looking down from above. So, I started to consider:

- Our time scale seems to be measured in terms of B.C. or A.D., Before Christ or Anno Domini. If the man Jesus was of no significance, why do we use him as a time reference?
- Why do children only need to be taught how to be good? How is it that they already know how to be bad? Who taught them?
- Being bad is easy, but being good is hard.
- New Age teaches that when you are living out your destiny, everything goes well for you. When you live contrary to your destiny, things do not go well. What or who, then, is controlling and directing our destiny? The powers of Darkness are the real-world Rulers. The real fight is behind the scenes in the spiritual realm.

*Ephesians 6 verse 12 says: - For we are not contending against flesh and blood, but against the principalities and against powers of darkness, against world rulers of this present darkness.*

Upon my return to Sydney, I visited Rodney, the old Kung Fu master. Since this whole thing started with his introducing me to the Togakure Ryu; it seemed fitting that if I was going to retire, I should pay him one last visit.

He mentioned in conversation about some kids in Bankstown who tried to summon demons. They went to the church grounds and made a circle of rocks, which, if unbroken, would protect them from the demons. They started inside the circle, reading the Bible backward; suddenly, something very big and powerful appeared. The kids, terrified, stepped backward and broke the circle of rocks, at which point they were attacked. Running from the church grounds, they all headed for the local police station. One kid had what seemed to be claw marks on his arm. The police had some trouble believing their story and locked them up for smoking pot. The fact is, if what was written in the Bible was just a bunch of words, why was it being used in an occult ceremony? Why did that need to take place on the grounds of a church?

Not long after returning to Australia, I had another out-of-body experience in my sleep. I found myself travelling down a series of passages and eventually arriving at a very long passage, at the end of which was something that radiated pure evil, with a face like a goat and a long snout, dark green in colour. A sense of absolute fear gripped me as I was drawn to this thing like a magnet.

In the middle of the attack, I said: " In the name of the Father, the Son," and I meant to say Holy Ghost, but I suddenly found myself wide awake, sitting upright in bed with a sense of peace. Never again would I be attacked in this way.

I now had an undeniable gut feeling that to be permanently free from demonic forces, I had to find a church. Since I was taught to insist on reality, I now knew what reality was: Jesus Christ crucified. The church would become my sanctuary.

I visited many different churches but found myself getting bored to death. So, I discovered which church my doctor friend attended, a Pentecostal church. They had a band with guitars and a keyboard instead of an organ. The music sounded pretty good, and it was a lively kind of place. More than that, it made me feel sick to go there. If I were demonically oppressed and there was any truth in the church, then I should feel sick. The moment I left the church building, I immediately felt better. I am forever amazed that when I am unsure about a direction in life, the devil always comes along with some encouragement.

So, I stayed in the Christian Growth Centre, and when the chi was present, I felt strong, but after a church service, I always felt weak. Thus, when I was strong, I was really weak, and when I was weak, I was really strong. Every Sunday, I went to church, and I felt great resistance. The more resistance I felt, the more determined I became. This continued for six months until the sickness was replaced by a sense of peace.

Around this time, I became involved in Wednesday night prayer meetings at the doctor's place. They always concluded with each individual being prayed for. This doctor was a prophet of God and would make statements or express insights while praying over you. The prophecies made over me were things I discussed with no one. These words could only come from someone who knew my every thought: God.

One Sunday, I saw an old woman with two walking sticks and someone helping her walk out the front for healing. After some prayer, she returned to her chair without the walking sticks. She staggered a little, but she was cured.

There was power in the church.

In the Church, it was possible to receive the Baptism of the Holy Spirit, also known as Holy Fire. Once you had this baptism, the more you prayed, the happier and more at peace you became. The Holy Fire is the source of all supernatural phenomena in the church. Just as the serpent fire or chi is on the dark side of life, so the Holy Fire is on the light side of life. However, the Holy Fire isn't trying to kill you, but rather to comfort you. Do you think anyone in the church could appreciate that? Martial Artists train three to four hours a day to possess great skills; many Christians would be lucky to pray for fifteen minutes a day.

I've also discovered that the more I read the Bible, the more my character transforms. I can read a verse in Proverbs repeatedly and gain new insights each time, proving that there are lessons within lessons. Moreover, I found that reading the gospel (Matthew, Mark, Luke, and John) often brought tears to my eyes while simultaneously softening my heart. It was the Love of Jesus entering my heart and softening it. Martial Arts Schools seem focused on hardening the heart, and in no school I ever attended did I see any love.

A soft heart is pliable, while a hard heart will be broken.

> *But God, being so very rich in mercy, because of His great and wonderful love with which He loved me. Even while I was dead, and separated from Him because of my sins, He made me alive.* (Eph 2:4)

## DAVID COZZ – DELTA FORCE

Not long after I left martial arts, David Cozz started his own martial arts organisation called Wind Warriors, based in Spokane, Washington. It was more of a cult, as every member had to adhere to strict discipline. Control is a central theme in all cults. Members were required to maintain part-time jobs to accommodate full-time training, which lasted eight hours a day. They also had to follow strict diets, maintain rigorous exercise schedules, and dedicate a significant portion of their day to meditation. This level of discipline produced some truly tough warriors. What equivalent practices do we find in Christianity?

By the way, David Cozz died of an aneurysm at age fifty. His great skill could not save him from a premature death, nor did he die with the knowledge of Christ.

## RODNEY HALL – KUNG FU

Another important lesson can be drawn from the old Kung Fu master. Many years after dedicating my life to Christ, I googled Rodney's name one day, and a mobile number appeared, so I called it. At that time, Rodney was living in West Ryde (a western suburb of Sydney), which was on my way home from work. I decided to drop by on my way home. There was the great Sifu (Teacher), dying from bowel cancer. He spent his days searching the original Hebrew and Greek of the Bible, looking for what to expect after his death. But at night, he used a machine to try to invoke an out-of-body experience, aiming to get a glimpse behind the scenes of what to expect. My first shock was that, despite his background and knowledge, he had never had an out-of-body experience. The second shock was that, even though he knew my story and had a hand in it, he was still reaching out for his own experience.

For most of the year that followed, I visited him once a week, sometimes at home and sometimes in the hospital. In his quest for his own out-of-body experience, he discovered two types of people. The first group claimed that astral travel is harmless and that everyone should try it. They encourage as many people as possible to participate. The second group maintained that the moment they found themselves outside their body, a demon was waiting to enter and take possession. This group sought to discourage anyone from engaging in astral travel.

When I was offered a job in town, I went to see Rodney and told him I might not be dropping in much anymore. He had a breakthrough. He recalled being out of his body and in what seemed like an underground cave. He remembered turning a corner, and whatever happened next was so horrific that his mind blocked it out, leaving him unable to remember. The following week would be my last to visit, and this time, Rodney was different. He was once again the great sifu, with pride and vanity filling his voice. Then the Lord spoke to me in a small, still voice: "He has a spirit of confusion, and if you stay longer, it will leap onto you." I left and never saw him again. Looking back on this, I have the same question you probably have: "Why didn't God just get me to cast it out?" I honestly don't know. It might not have been as straightforward as you and I are thinking.

# Journey into Light

Once I established myself at the Christian Growth Centre I blended in with several groups. Two of these were really good house churches, led by well-established leaders. Then there was the Friday night group.

## The Friday Night Group

A group of guys who grew up in the church would meet every Friday to enjoy a six-pack of beer and watch horror movies. I thought it was all harmless fun until one night when I had a dream about watching a horror movie, and something jumped out of the screen and attacked me. If watching a horror movie could open me up to demonic influence, how much more could that happen when combined with alcohol? Within ten years, many members of that group were no longer following the Lord..

*Small deviation in the way, over time, leads to large deviation in the way.* [4]

## THE HOUSE

God blessed me early in my walk by giving me the opportunity to buy my first house. Little did I know that Sydney property prices would appreciate to the point of becoming unaffordable in just a few short years.

Not long after moving in, I began to envision how the house could be renovated and how to transform a two-bedroom house into three. I was working long hours at my job, only to come home and spend additional long hours renovating. There was no time for God. The real problem was that I didn't recognize I had a problem. One night, I dreamed I was a World War II POW, working on an abandoned Spitfire that required engine repairs. I had ideas to fix the engine and fly the plane out of camp. However, each night, the enemy would come and take some parts from the engine, ensuring I never got it to work but laboured in vain.

The entire house renovation was a strategy of the devil to ensure I didn't grow in Christ and didn't have time for God. A short time later, a property developer began buying up houses in the street, offering everyone the same price, regardless of what renovations had been made.

It's very important, when receiving ideas and visions, that you don't necessarily attribute them to God. Ask yourself, "What does it achieve?" "Does this tree bear good fruit or bad?" "Do I have enough resources to complete this task?" Then, ask God in prayer to show you what is going on behind the scenes.

## Tongues

One day, without prompting, words started coming into my head. Words that weren't really words. More like gobble gook. As I said each word, I experienced an emotional release and a sense of warmth. A friend from church called it praying in tongues. But no one had laid hands upon me. I also discovered that there is a demonic tongue. How do I know what I had? So, for eighteen months, I did not pray in tongues.

I found that when I prayed in tongues, I was drawing closer to God, not further away. Would a demonic tongue bring me closer to God? I therefore concluded it was a heavenly tongue and entered a period where I prayed in tongues at every opportunity I could. While this was edifying, without grounding in the Word of God, it creates the super spiro who can't discern between God's voice and their own thoughts.

## The Word

I started reading my Bible. I actually read it from cover to cover. To my surprise, most Christians had not done this. The story of God delivering His people from Egyptian slavery and leading them into the promised land spoke volumes to me about a typical Christian life. We were all slaves to sin and were delivered with great deliverance.

There were times when the Israelites forsook the Lord their God and followed other gods, only for the Lord to intervene and bring them back to Him. Then I came to the Psalms and Proverbs. It was poetry. I'm a bloke, and we don't do poetry. But wisdom is justified by her children.

Many years would pass before I truly understood that the power of the Word of God is found in meditating on the Word.

## Bad Gifts

I had two friends: Jerry, an American from Minnesota, and Alex, an Australian working as an explosives expert for a mining company in New Guinea. Jerry had sent me two knives as gifts, and one in particular that I was fond of had a handle made from the jaw of a bear.

A short time later, Alex arrived at my doorstep during one of his breaks, carrying a bow and arrow set with arrows dipped in pigs' blood as a form of poison. To accompany the bow and arrow set was a shield topped with a carved head. It looked hideous. Not wanting to offend, I accepted the gifts.

Some time went by, and a Christian girl I was dating came over for dinner. She noticed the shield and immediately claimed that there was a dark presence attached to it. To make her happy, I took the shield, along with the bow and arrow set, out of the house and into the garage. This produced an immediate change in the atmosphere. The next day, I completely removed the artifacts from my property.

I was now curious about the knives, so I took them to someone I knew who had a vast knowledge of occult practices. He confirmed that those particular knives were used in the rituals of the American Indians. As a result, I disposed of the knives.

Having occult artifacts in my house gave the devil a foothold to take up residence. Now that the artifacts have been removed, I proceeded through each room in the house and prayerfully kicked out all the demons I had allowed in.

## Weeding the Garden

*And some fell among thorns and the thorns sprang up and choked them.* (Matt 13:7)

I must have read this passage more than a dozen times before I realized it was talking about me. We all live busy lives. There are demands from business, from our jobs, and from our families, along with social pressures, including the church. As organizations try to do more with less, there is increasing pressure from employers to require more from their employees. There simply isn't time to do everything.

These are the cares of this world that choke the seed and ensure you don't have time in your busy day for God. This can take the form of a ministry. When a minister puts his ministry above his relationship with God, he begins to lose his first love, and the anointing leaves him, as it did with King Saul. He believes that what he is doing is in service to God, but it is not. Just like the Pharisees of old. They thought they were serving God, but they deceived themselves, lacking a true relationship. If this problem is not addressed, the end result is burnout or, worse, falling away from the Lord.

Each day, no matter how many worldly issues you are dealing with, you need to set aside time with God to nurture this relationship. Your predominant thoughts will be those that spring out of your heart. Your predominant thoughts that you think need to be of or about God. God needs to be number one on a list of one.

## Healing of the Memories

After getting married and moving to a large Pentecostal Church, I felt there were spiritual blockages. I turned to a Christian counsellor who understood the healing of the memories. With him, I sat down and made a list of everyone who had sinned against me. To my surprise, this list was only one page long. However, I was holding some significant issues against my father. Only after forgiving him did I understand that releasing him also released me to worship my Father in heaven with true intimacy, such as the Father desires.

Forgiving my earthly father opened a greater relationship with my heavenly Father. The result was nothing short of wonderful.

## MEDITATING ON PSALMS

I decided to join the church's 6:00 am prayer meeting, led by a woman named Alice. It was a small group, so there was no worship. Instead, we would pray through a psalm before calling out to God with our prayers and petitions.

When the prayer meetings eventually came to a close, I tried to incorporate a meditation on Psalms into my morning ritual to deepen my connection with God. The results seemed mixed, almost dependent on which side of the bed I got out of.

I realized that my mind often drifted off subject. One thought led to another, typically related to work or family. As I examined this trail of thoughts, a theme emerged that could be described as an emotion. For example, if I needed to present something for work, I found myself preoccupied with the task and what I needed to do to prepare. This was driven by fear. If I had recently experienced a falling out with my wife and felt she was genuinely in the wrong, that would manifest as anger.

Regardless of the emotion and circumstances, it blocked me from God.

Recognizing the blockage, I concentrated on the emotion at hand and observed until it shifted. If the emotion changes and anger transforms into fear, I then focus on the fear. Eventually, I found peace, having purged the negativity. Only then did I realize that at the core of my being is someone who just wants to worship the God that created him.

This is my proverb: Learn from the toilet. Doesn't the whole body feel better after you purge the crap.

You are now ready to start meditating on Psalms. Let's consider Psalm 100:3 as an example. *"Know that the Lord is God. It is He Who made us, and we are His; we are His people, the sheep of His pasture"*.

"He who made us." You mean we didn't evolve from a caterpillar? We were, in fact, created. Created by Him. Should I not be thankful for my very life? We are "His people." What a great privilege. Those who say "we are his people" are few on the earth. Should I not be grateful? We are the "sheep of his pasture." What pasture? The earth is his pasture. He made it for us to dwell in. We are His sheep, and the shepherd looks after His sheep. What can I possibly articulate in thanks that would give all the glory He is due?

I usually look for Psalms that glorify God. I don't try to read the whole Psalm, but meditate on just a few verses that I can use to glorify Him. Sometimes, I would spend weeks on one verse. The result is a level of worship where every fibre of my being is engaged in worshipping Him. I find no greater pleasure than this.

Is there anything more right than the thing made should worship He that made it?

## Meditating on Proverbs

Zen archers meditate on Chinese riddles, and by doing so, they can hit their targets blindfolded. How much more will the spirit of God flow through us when we meditate on Proverbs?

Proverbs describes the plight of three losers: the scoffer, the fool, and the simple. At any given moment, we can find ourselves in one of these three groups. A successful life consists of making the right choices. I personally have made too many wrong choices. The homeless man begging in the street isn't there because he is evil; he's there because he made a series of poor choices, to which we are all susceptible.

So, I turned to the book of Proverbs.

Take the principles I used to meditate on Psalms and apply them to Proverbs. Let's consider Proverb 25:16: *"Have you found honey? Take only what you need, lest you be full of it and vomit"*.

So, if you eat too much honey, you get sick and vomit. That makes sense. But what if the author wasn't talking about honey? Am I the only one who has drunk too much wine and vomited? A little wine is good, while a lot of wine is not good. So, the proverb outlines a principle that can be applied to many different areas of life. The book is a multi-dimensional book. But what was the author really referring to? To find the answer, you must look at where else honey is used in Proverbs. In most cases, it refers to glory. Self-glorification isn't glorifying.

So, the proverb should read: have you found glory and honour, take only what you need lest you be full of yourself and speak vanity. Notice it says, "Take only what you need." We are all due and in need of some honour and recognition. But don't let it go to your head.

I found that meditating on Proverbs changed the way I thought. I started to see and consider other people's points of view. I began to think more deeply about issues, whereas previously, I would look for and accept the simplest reasoning for a problem. For example, the simplest view to explain cancer is "it's just another infirmity caused by a spirit of infirmity." There are cases where that's true, but in most cases, it is not, and numerous environmental factors contribute to the development of cancerous growth. There are hundreds of different cancers, each with different causes, and each individual's immune system plays a part. The problem is complex. The answer is often also complex one.

> *How long will you simple ones, will you love simplicity* (Prov 1:22)

## Proverbs Chapter Seven

While meditating on Proverbs, I came across chapter seven. It was all to do with a seductress. I wasn't a lustful individual. Was there any Bible verse less relevant to me than this one?

> *With her enticing speech, she caused him to yield, with her flattering lips she seduced him. Immediately he went after her, as an ox goes to the slaughter.* (Prov 7:22)

Henry Cloud, the author of a famous book called "Boundaries," was in Sydney to promote a new book titled "The Mum Factor." I purchased a copy and, while reading, was immediately drawn to chapter three, "The Phantom Mum." The phantom mum is never present when the child needs a hug and a little reassurance. It produces a son who, when he marries, views his wife as the love object and the office girl (or whoever catches his eye) as the sex object. This leads to an affair that destroys the marriage. He then wonders where the love object went. [5]

Now, we have an entire generation rising up where both parents work. The kids' physical needs are met, but not their emotional needs. Infidelity and divorce are at all-time highs and continuing to increase.

Was chapter seven relevant? For me, the scariest verse in the Bible is this: *By means of a harlot, a man is reduced to a crust of bread.* (Prov 6:26)

It was not a question of whether Satan would use this strategy on me, but when he might use this strategy.

Looking back on my life, I suspect the only reason Satan has not attempted this strategy is that I am constantly vigilant in watching out for this scheme. When you're not looking for it, you are vulnerable.

## MEDITATING ON EPHESIANS

My wife and I were serving in a community church run by a Māori woman named Josie Parata, who had been diagnosed with stage four breast cancer and advised by doctors to get her affairs in order. By faith, she stood on the word, and in doing so, she was miraculously healed, which shocked the doctors. A true warrior for Christ. Thanks to Josie, when the evangelist Tim Hall began a series of tent meetings in Sydney, we were fortunate to become involved. We were invited to some training workshops led by Tim.

This would turn out to be my final step into light.

Tim's aim was to equip us with faith ahead of the upcoming meeting. To achieve this, he provided each participant with a copy of his book "Armed and Dangerous". It is truly a great book, well worth the read. Tim encouraged us to meditate on the book of Ephesians, particularly two prayers Paul prays on behalf of the Ephesians. He recommended conducting an exegesis expository on these two prayers to grasp the deep meaning of what has been said and to pray that over ourselves daily. I used "Ephesian An Exegetical Commentary" by Harold W Hoehner to research the actual Greek wording. I would highly recommend it to anyone who wants a deep understanding.

First prayer in the original NJKV version:

> Eph 1:17 I pray that the God of our Lord Jesus Christ, the Father of glory, may grant you a spirit of wisdom and of revelation into the true knowledge of Him. And that

the eyes of your heart may be enlightened, so that you will know and cherish the hope to which He has called you, the riches of his glorious inheritance and what is the immeasurable and unlimited and surpassing greatness of His power in us who believe.

First prayer modified, explanatory version that I prayed:

> Eph 1:17 O magnificent God, father of our Lord Jesus Christ, the king of glory, I ask for a spirit of wisdom, insight into how things really are, and insight into how people really are. I pray for a spirit of revelation, deep, Intimate insight into who you are. I pray that you would flood my heart with the light of your Holy Spirit so that I might know the magnitude of my calling and the rich inheritance I have in you. That I might know and understand the immeasurable, unlimited, surpassing power that is in me and flows through me as a child of God as part of my inheritance that is here and now, and not just set aside for a future time.

Second prayer in the original NJKV version:

> Eph 3:16 that He would grant you, according to the riches of His glory, to be strengthened with might through His Spirit in the inner man, that Christ may dwell in your hearts through faith; that you, being rooted and grounded in love, may be able to comprehend with all the saints what is the width and length and depth and height to know the love of Christ which passes knowledge; that you may be filled with all fullness of God.

Second prayer modified, explanatory version that I prayed:

> Eph: 3:16 Father, I ask that You grant out of the riches of Your great glory that I will be strengthened and spiritually energised with active power through Your Spirit in my inner man, so that Christ himself may dwell in my heart through faith. And that I might be rooted and firmly grounded in love. And that I might know and comprehend the width, length, height, and depth of the love of Christ. Come fill me to overflowing with your divine presence.

After meditating extensively on the book of Ephesians, these were my findings:

The book is a highly mystical book. Full of knowledge that's beyond knowing. You can know it in your heart, but you can't get it in your head. We are finite beings trying to comprehend an infinite God. The first three chapters have to do with instruction. The second three chapters have to do with duty. What to do with that instruction.

For most of my Christian life, I've been happy with just eternal life. The idea of not spending eternity in Sheol really appeals to me. But the salvation of Christ is far more wonderful than we can ever hope or wish for.

> *He predestined and lovingly planned for us to be adopted to Himself as His own children.* (Eph 1:5)

Who is "He"? God. Which God? The great God. The God who created over two trillion galaxies, each with over a billion stars, just so that when man looks into the heavens, he could see the glory of God. The God who loves you more than your mother ever did or could. That God predestined you before the beginning of time to be adopted into His family. If you're adopted, then you have an inheritance. The very power that raised Christ from the dead is working in you and through you for His great purposes. This inheritance isn't for a future time, it's for here and now.

Moreover, we are meant to be in fellowship and union with Christ himself. That union reflects the depth of intimacy one might associate with a husband and wife. Have you ever raised your hands in worship and felt the tangible presence of God? The peace of God. The love of God. That's just a small taste of things to come. The greatest thing about Christ's salvation is not merely eternal life but the fellowship and union with Christ Himself.

If you can get this into you, you will be UNSTOPPABLE.

## The War on Three Fronts

If you are born again, you are born into a war. It's a war few of us are prepared for. This book will hopefully help to prepare you for the times to come. We war on three fronts:

- The flesh (self)
- The world
- The devil

Of the three adversaries, Self has proven to be the most difficult.

# PART II

## The Way of the Flesh

*If anyone would come after me, let him deny himself and take up his cross daily and follow me. (Luke 9:23)*

# Me Myself and I

When I got saved I didn't pray "Lord save me from the devil" I prayed "Lord save me from ME".

The greatest thing stopping me from being all I can be in Christ, is ME. If you have read chapter two, you will know I've had some challenges from the devil. But this adversary (Me) is far more problematic. "I don't want to get out of bed in the morning." "I want to eat all the wrong foods." "I don't want to go to work today." "I want to drink a beer while I watch footy." I want, I want, and I want.

*The eyes of man are never satisfied (Prov 27:20)*

We are, by nature, creatures that try to avoid pain and suffering and gravitate towards pleasure. This gravitation towards pleasure is what the Bible refers to as lusts of the flesh. The battle is a battle of the mind.

> *For the flesh lusts against the Spirit, and the Spirit against the flesh; and these are contrary to one another so that you do not do the things that you wish. (Galatians 5:17)*

Our selfish desires war against the will of God. Spiritual Warfare begins with the Self.

> *For we know that the law is spiritual, but I am of the flesh, sold under sin. For I do not understand my own actions. For I do not do what I want, but I do the very thing I hate. Now if I do what I do not want, I agree with the law, that it is good. So now it is no longer I who do it, but sin that dwells within me. For I know that nothing good dwells in me, that is, in my flesh. For I have the desire to do what is right, but not the ability to carry it out. For I do not do the good I want, but the evil I do not want is what I keep on doing. Now if I do what I do not want, it is no longer I who do it, but sin that dwells within me.*
>
> *So, I find it to be a law that when I want to do right, evil lies close at hand. For I delight in the law of God, in my inner being, but I see in my members another law waging war against the law of my mind and making me captive to the law of sin that dwells in my members. Wretched man that I am! Who will deliver me from this body of death? Thanks be to God through Jesus Christ our Lord! So then, I myself serve the law of God with my mind, but with my flesh I serve the law of sin. (Rom 7:14-25)*

Romans chapter seven reveals the warfare that a true believer faces with the flesh while striving to live that resurrection life, a common theme in the epistles. Let's now consider some of the barriers we are likely to face.

### BARRIERS TO BEING CHRIST-LIKE

There are numerous aspects that will block you from being Christ-like. Let's look at those that are specific to Self.

Broadly, these blockages fall into four categories:

- Ignorance – is ignorant of who we are in Christ
- Wrong Choices that are disobedience to God
- New Wine in an Old Wineskin
- Blindness – This is spiritual blindness, which we will deal with in the next chapter

## *Ignorance*

Ignorance takes two forms:

- Not knowing who God is
- Not knowing who we are in Christ

> *But he who is careless of his ways will die* (Prov 19:16)

We cannot afford to be careless in our way. If we are ignorant of who God is, then we don't have a relationship with Him. We turn up to church on Sundays out of duty and view salvation as an escape from sin's judgment. Not knowing who we are in Christ is a lesser problem than not knowing God. Without knowing who we are, we are disempowered from walking in the authority of Christ and taking dominion over the enemy. We become ineffective in the battle.

Both of these problems have the same solution. Meditating on the Word of God will renew your heart and mind. It is this renewing process that transforms us from being flesh-like to being Christ-like. Jesus Christ is the model we are all meant to mimic.

## *Wrong Choices*

Wrong choices can lead us to knowingly or unknowingly sin. A successful life is made up of having made the right choices.

> *If any of you lack wisdom, let him ask of God, that giveth to all men liberally, and without reproach and it shall be given to him.* (James 1:5)

In my early days of martial arts, I became deeply connected with Eastern wisdom and thought I was wise. In reality, I was deluded. The wisdom of the East had no substance to it. There were no consequences for having gotten it wrong. The wisdom that the Bible offers, on the other hand, is great and awesome and will save your soul from destruction.

> *Fear of the Lord is the beginning of Wisdom* (Prov 9:10)

Wisdom begins with fearing the Lord rather than fearing man or worrying about what others might think of you. Meditating on the book of Proverbs, as I did, is an excellent way to solve the wrong choice problem. However, as I've journeyed into the Bible, I'm finding that proverbs are a type of baby wisdom and that deeper wisdom lies in what Jesus said and did.

If you need wisdom (and you deceive yourself if you think you don't), begin by asking God. Then, start meditating on the book of Proverbs. Not a chapter a day; try focusing on just one or two verses. Ask yourself, how does this apply to me? Could the subjects be idioms for something else? What principle does this scripture communicate, and how can I apply that to my life? Let the Word transform your heart, and you will see that it will change the way you think and perceive the world.

## *New Wine in an Old Wine Skin*

While you were separated from God, your worldly experiences deeply ingrained thought patterns, memories, responses, and habits that diverge from God's ways. Thus, even though your old self has vanished, your flesh still opposes God due to a preprogrammed tendency toward sin, and living apart from Him.

To shed the old wine skin, you need to forget your old views and start to consider new ones. Stop thinking you know something and don't need to learn it again. Is your view the only view? How accurate is that view? Do I know all the facts? It's a wise prayer to ask the Father to show you patterns of thinking that are stopping you from learning something new. It is very typical of the Father to want to do and teach a new thing.

## *Shedding the Old Wine Skin*

These eight steps will assist you in shedding your old wine skin and positioning yourself to receive the Word of God. These are the steps I took in healing the memories as described in chapter three. They will address both conscious and sometimes unconscious bitterness, shame, rejection, and negative emotions that have been planted from past events and are holding you back.

The steps that follow are not easy, but they require courage, as they will remove any remaining blockages you have from communing with the God who loves you. They will also eliminate footholds the devil is using to gain access to your heart.

1. Make a list of everyone who has hurt you from as far back as you can remember. List the people involved and what they did to you.
2. Express any negative feelings instead of suppressing them. Start by finding a safe, controlled place where you can just let your emotions fly out without impacting others. Suppressing these deep feelings only leads to damaging emotions popping out when people press the right buttons. This only increases your inner shame.
3. Accept your responsibility for your negative, hateful feelings.
4. Ask yourself if you really want to be healed of your emotions and past hurts. Not everyone is ready to forgive. It takes time to mentally process the event, generate all the emotions that stem from that event, and then act contrary to your thoughts and feelings.
5. By faith, choose to forgive all those who have hurt you. Sit down with someone you trust and prayerfully go through your list, forgiving each offender as you go.
6. Choose to forgive yourself and ask God to forgive you. Even though you are the victim, you will need to ask God to forgive you for holding on to this unforgiveness.
7. After forgiving an offender, ask Him to heal you of this event. Prayerfully ask the Lord to heal your heart, mind, and emotions so you might be in perfect health.
8. Break any footholds of Satan in your life that resulted from the abuser. Prayerfully removes any foothold that the devil has accessed due to this event.

## Self Centeredness

The worst kind of problem is the problem we are not aware of. We are all self-centred to varying degrees and at different times. This is a deep-rooted behaviour we learned as kids. It breaks down into two steps: what we think and what we do. Covetousness is born from our thoughts and desires, what we think. I am not to say we can't have healthy desires, but healthy desires tend to reflect a benefit for someone else. In that instance, we are not self-centred.

> *Do nothing out of selfish ambition or vain conceit but in humility consider others better than yourselves.* (Phil 2:3)

I have attended many Christian conferences at large venues where you have to wait and queue up for sometimes hours just to get in and find a seat. It's just like going to a rock concert. The key difference is that there is less pushing and shoving at a rock concert. Okay, I might have exaggerated a bit on the last illustration. But I think you understand my point. People who call themselves followers and disciples of Jesus are looking after their own needs ahead of their fellow believers. My God, please help these people.

> *Whoever wants to be my disciple must deny themselves and take up their cross daily and follow me* (Luke 9:23)

Denying ourselves is the complete opposite of what the world will tell you to do. Have you seen how much we are daily bombarded with advertisements on our phones, on our TVs, and on our computers? The ads are rarely informative, always trying to sell you what you don't need. Do you have the latest iPhone? iPhone 99 makes anything you view on the web seem like you are really there. It can transport you anywhere, anytime. We'll talk about misinformation from the media in another section of this book.

Selflessness is a moment-by-moment choice. We can choose to be selfless or to give in to selfishness. If we are all selfish by nature, then it is natural for us to choose ourselves first, above others. Since we are born into a sinful, fallen world, we are born into a selfish world.

Stopping selfishness takes a conscientious effort to shift our focus away from ourselves, stop the constant desire for self-gratification, and put others ahead of ourselves, situation by situation, day after day. Carrying your cross and dying to yourself needs to be done daily.

Selfishness is the root cause of all sin. [6]

## Self Control

> *Like a city whose walls are broken down is a man who lacks self-control.* (Prov 25:28)

Self-control involves learning to manage impulses and delaying gratification. We all struggle with this in certain areas of our lives. Self-control and self-discipline are essential for living a Christ-like life. Can an athlete win a race without training? Can they train without self-discipline and self-control? What about a new recruit in the army? How long would they last without self-control and self-discipline?[6]

The key to self-control is managing your emotions. Once we lose emotional control, we give power to those around us, those who are in conflict with us, and those with whom we have a relationship. This usually results in us saying or doing something we regret later. The scenario becomes a playground for the devil.

When you are verbally attacked, you have a choice to react or respond. When you react, you return demeaning comments in exchange for demeaning statements made about you. This only escalates the argument.

> *A soft answer turns away wrath, but a harsh word stirs up anger. (Prov 15:1)*

The first step to self-control is to monitor your emotions and not let them rise to the point where you can't control them. If you see you are starting to lose control, then walk away and cool off. Don't give a foothold for the devil. Reconvene the conversation without the over-emotional content.

Another approach to self-control is to avoid placing yourself in situations where you may compromise your control. Avoid environments that present opportunities to lose your self-control. When you find yourself in such compromising situations, pray for strength and self-control in advance. As self-control is a skill developed over time, you will become stronger and less likely to falter under pressure.

True strength is found in conquering yourself, not in conquering someone else. Selfishness can't be conquered without self-control.

## Unconditional Love

Unconditional love means loving while expecting nothing in return. It is easy to love those who love you. However, unconditional love involves loving those who do not necessarily love you—those who speak harshly to you and those who hate you without cause. God loved us long before we loved him, as seen in Ephesians chapter two.

> *But God, who is rich in mercy, because of His great love with which He loved us, even when we were dead in trespasses, made us alive together with Christ. (Eph 2:4-5)*

When we were dead in our trespasses, not looking for God, not considering God, and having no thanks for our very existence, He loved us and chose us to be sons and daughters of God.

The ultimate expression of love can be found in Jesus' Crucifixion. While hanging there in agony, gasping for breath, Jesus says these words: "Father, forgive them for what they do." I have not found a greater expression of God's love.

To walk in unconditional love is not easy. We must deny ourselves, for starters. We should forgive those who sin against us and love others no matter their response. This is impossible for man, but all things are possible with God. We need revelation from His word about His love for us. Meditating on the following scriptures will help.

> *But God shows his love for us in that while we were still sinners, Christ died for us. (Rom 5:8)*

> *For God so loved the world, that he gave his only Son, that whoever believes in him should not perish but have eternal life. (John 3:16)*

> *So we have come to know and to believe the love that God has for us. God is love, and whoever abides in love abides in God, and God abides in him. (1 John 4:16)*

> *See what kind of love the Father has given to us, that we should be called children of God; and so we are. The reason why the world does not know us is that it did not know him. (1 John 3:1)*

> *But God, being rich in mercy, because of the great love with which he loved us, even when we were dead in our trespasses, made us alive together with Christ—by grace you have been saved (Eph 2:4-5)*

*Greater love has no one than this, that someone lay down his life for his friends. (John 15:13)*

*In this the love of God was made manifest among us, that God sent his only Son into the world, so that we might live through him. In this is love, not that we have loved God but that he loved us and sent his Son to be the propitiation for our sins. (1 John 4:9-10)*

# Spiritual Blindness

Spiritual Blindness is one of the greatest problems facing the church today. It affects all of us to some degree. If we are spiritually blind, then we are blind to the fact that we have a problem.

*For he who lacks these things is shortsighted, even to blindness.* (2 Peter 1:9)

In the Bible verse above, Peter is talking about believers who have become short-sighted and even blind, forgetting who they are and why they are here. Have you noticed that twenty percent of the congregation does eighty percent of the work? Many of the others show up for church on a Sunday and then immediately return to a worldly life for the rest of the week. Equally shocking is the unbeliever. They know they were born, and they know they will die. Shouldn't they be asking the question: "Where do we go from here?"

The problem of spiritual blindness can be best understood by two opposing states of mind. **In the Box** and **Out of the Box**.

## The Box

**In the Box**, we don't see the world as it is; we see the world as we are. We see people as objects, and in the worst case, as objects of inconvenience. We go through a process of self-justification to justify our actions and view of the world. People who agree with our worldview we consider allies, and those who oppose our worldview we consider adversaries. [7]

*A man's ways are right in his own eyes.* (Prov 21:2)

The following table describes the differences between these two states of mind.

| In the Box | Out of the Box |
|---|---|
| We see the world as we are | We see the world as it is |
| We see people as objects | We see people as people |
| We are only interested in what benefits us | We are interested in the welfare of others |
| We are interested in protecting our position & reputation | We are interested in the reputation of our team & organisation |
| We don't see when we have a problem | We are open to correction & constructive criticism |

Table 5.1 – In the Box versus Out of the Box

**Out Of The Box** we see people as people. We see the needs of the people around us and are empowered to help those people. We see situations in an unbiased way. We are open to instruction and correction.

**Out Of The Box** does not mean you become a "YES" man. If someone is trying to persuade you to do their job for them, then they are **In The Box** and if you are **Out Of The Box** you can choose to help if you have time and choose not to help if you do not.

A **Yes** while **In The Box** will have a negative tone and unfriendly body language. At the same time, a **No** while **Out Of The Box** will have a positive tone and unbiased body language.

Consider this example of being **In The Box**. My wife and I are fast asleep in bed. Our daughter, who is just eleven months old, wakes up crying. These are the thoughts that go through my head:

1. The baby is crying again
2. I feel like I should get up and tend to her
3. I've been working hard; I need my sleep
4. I can't believe she (my wife) is not budging
5. She's so lazy
6. What kind of Mum just lets her kid cry
7. She's obviously faking it

The first thought identifies the problem. The baby is crying. The second thought "I feel like I should get up", but I don't. At this point, I've betrayed myself and entered the Box.

The third thought, "I've been working hard and need my sleep" is a self-justifying thought to justify my inactivity. Have I really been working hard? Maybe my wife has been working harder. Through my self-justifying view, I'm beginning to see things in a distorted way.

The fourth thought, "I can't believe she's not budging" is making an assumption that my wife is awake and choosing to ignore the crying baby. Say, isn't that what I'm doing?

The fifth thought, "She's so lazy", is a judgment based on my distorted view of the situation. A judgment without knowing all the facts.

The sixth thought, "What kind of Mum lets her kid cry?". What kind of dad lets his kid cry is a greater truth.

The seventh thought, "She's obviously faking it", is an assumption and a judgment without knowing all the facts.

The judgments I had against my wife are the very judgments that reside against me, and the truth is not in me.

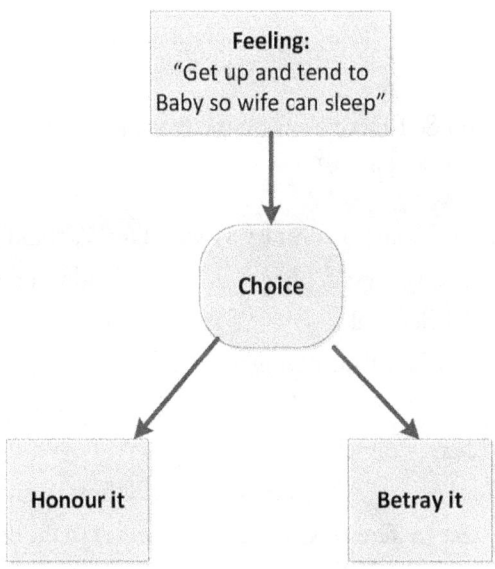

Figure 5.1 – The choice, honour or betray

When I first got the feeling to get up and tend to the baby, I had a choice. I could honour the feeling or betray it.[7]

By betraying my initial feeling, I created the following distorted view.

| How I started to see myself | How I started to see my wife |
|---|---|
| Victim | Lazy |
| Hardworking | Inconsiderate |
| Important | Unappreciative |
| Fair | Insensitive |
| Sensitive | Faker |
| Good Dad | Lousy Mum |
| Good Husband | Lousy Wife |

Table 5.2 – Distorted views

Leadership and Self-Deception by the Arbinger Institute describes the following steps of Self-Betrayal:

- Self-betrayal is an act contrary to what I feel I should do for another
- When I betray myself, I begin to see the world in a way that justifies my self-betrayal
- When I see a self-justifying world, my view of reality becomes distorted
- When I betray myself, I enter the Box
- Over time, certain self-justifying views become part of my character
- When I act **In The Box**, I encourage others to do the same.[7]

When I betray myself, I enter the Box, and I become self-deceived:

- I inflate other people's faults
- I inflate my own virtues
- I inflate the values of things that justify my self-betrayal
- I look for someone to blame

Whenever my focus is inward, I act contrary to how I feel. I don't see the world as it is; I see the world as I am. This leads me to perceive the world in a distorted way, and the truth is not in me.

In the moment we cease resisting others, we're **Out Of The Box** and liberated from self-justifying thoughts and feelings.

Getting **Out Of The Box** starts with questioning the validity of your thoughts. Let's reconsider the baby-crying scenario. These are the thoughts that go through my head:

1. How do I know she's faking it?
2. What if she's really asleep?
3. Is she really lazy?
4. If she's asleep, then it's me that's faking it
5. She's not lazy, I am
6. I should really get up to the baby

The truth was that my wife wasn't faking it. This was the third night in a row where my wife had little or no sleep.

## *Final Comments*

We all suffer from being **In The Box** to some degree. Only when we are **Out Of The Box** can we see clearly what the needs around us are, and we are empowered to act. Make every effort to maintain an outward focus instead of an inward focus. This will help you avoid being **In The Box** and better position you to see in the spirit and engage in the battle.

Once you are **In The Box** you begin to see the world in a distorted way. You invite others to be **In The Box**, and the self-deception then spreads like a disease. **In the Box** you will be reading the Bible with a filtered view. The doctrine that aligns with your actions and way of life, you will accept.

The doctrine that challenges your view, you will tend to skip over as if it doesn't exist.

If you want to learn more about the Box and how being **In The Box** causes others to be **In The Box**, I'd recommend the book "Leadership and Self-Deception" by Arbinger Institute.[7] It's the best book I've read, next to the Bible.

Now that you understand how spiritual blindness manifests, let's have a look at some of the consequences of being **In The Box**.

## DISTORTIONS OF THE MIND

From an **In The Box** position, your view of the world is distorted in several well-defined ways. The following is a list of psychological distortions that you can expect from being **In The Box**:
- Overgeneralization
- Global Labelling
- Filtering
- Polarised Thinking
- Self-Blame
- Personalization
- Mind Reading
- Control Fallacies
- Emotional Reasoning [8]

## *Overgeneralization*

From one isolated event, you make a general rule. If you fail once, you'll always fail.

*Example*: You accidentally delete a file on your computer. Your thought response: "I'm technically incompetent".
*Impact on Self-Esteem*: Lowers self-esteem when directed at yourself.

## *Global Labelling*

You automatically use derogatory labels to describe yourself rather than accurately describing your qualities. This can also apply to a class of people, things, behaviours, and experiences.
*Example*: A guy in a work van cuts you off in traffic. Your thought response: "All people who drive work vans are arrogant morons"
*Impact on Self-Esteem*: Lowers self-esteem when directed at yourself.

## *Filtering*

When filtering, you focus on the negative aspects and ignore the positive ones.
*Example*: Your boss sits you down to give you a performance review. He has ten very positive aspects to highlight. But all you can think about is the one thing he didn't have a glowing report about.
*Impact on Self-Esteem*: This type of distortion can be very damaging to low self-esteem if the filter is filtering out all positive statements.

## *Polarised Thinking*

Polarised thinking categorises things as absolute, black-and-white, leaving no middle ground. You must be perfect, or you are deemed worthless.
*Example*: You hear a news report that domestic violence is on the rise. Your thought response: "Yes, too many men can't control their anger." This

thought does not allow for the possibility that it's a woman who could be the violent one.

*Impact on Self-Esteem*: This type of thinking can paint a very negative view of the world.

## Self-Blame

You consistently blame yourself for things that may not really be your fault.

*Example*: You're late for work. Your thought response: "If only I'd set the alarm earlier." When the reality is that the bus was late, the fault lies with the bus company.

*Impact on Self-Esteem*: This sort of thinking erodes self-esteem.

## Personalisation

Personalisation leads to negative comparisons with others, resulting in inappropriate behaviours.

*Example*: A friend says that he is bored, and you think he's bored with you.

*Impact on Self-Esteem*: Inappropriate reactions make you look foolish.

## Mind Reading

With Mind Reading, we often assume that others dislike us, are angry with us, or don't care about us, without substantial evidence to support these beliefs.

*Example:* I go to the office Monday morning, and the boss, who's usually very friendly, looks up and grunts and then goes back to work. Your thought response: "He is not happy with me." "Didn't he like the report I sent him last week?" The truth was that he was just hungover.

*Impact on Self-Esteem*: This distortion is detrimental for those with low self-esteem. If you have a negative view of yourself, you will likely assume that everyone else perceives you the same way.

## *Control Fallacies*

You either feel that you have total responsibility for everybody and everything, or you feel that you have no control, that you're a helpless victim. It's either over control or under control.

*Example*: The boss chews me out at work. I come home only to hear the wife scream, "You're late for dinner, again," while picking up the latest electricity bill from the table. Obviously, the boss, the wife, and the electricity company have colluded together just to make my day miserable.

*Impact on Self-Esteem*: Being under control affects self-esteem, leaving you feeling helpless.

## *Emotional Reasoning*

With emotional reasoning, you assume that things are the way you feel about them.

*Example*: You feel useless, so you must be useless.

*Impact on Self-Esteem*: On days you feel good, you have a can-do attitude. On days you feel down, you're no good for anything. It's a roller coaster ride.

## Correcting Distortions

As time goes by, these distorted ways of thinking become a part of our personality. It takes discipline to catch yourself out with one or more of these distortions. Once you catch the distortion, you can challenge it and correct your thinking and thereby guard your self-esteem.

If you realise you've entertained thoughts that were psychological distortions leading to labelling or judging others, now is the time to make it right.

Pray this prayer:

"Father, I thank you for being a gracious God, slow to anger and quick to forgive. Father, I ask that you forgive me for my wrong thinking and for judging others. Open the eyes of my understanding that I might see people as people and love them as you love them. Amen"

## Self Esteem

*Guard your heart for out of it spring the issues of life.*
(Prov 4:23)

There is much sin that stems from low self-esteem. Vanity psychologically compensates for low self-esteem. Vanity pushes God away. *God hates a proud eye and a lying tongue.* (Prov 6:17)

Low self-esteem serves as a foothold for the devil to manipulate your thinking. Once he has you thinking in negative terms, you enter a downward spiral. The devil doesn't have to do anything once he has you on that path. You are destined for depression. Depression not only creates inner pain that may lead to substance abuse, but it also disempowers you from fighting the good fight for Christ.

When a plane goes into a spiral spin, the pilot applies the left aileron and right rudder to pull the plane out of the spin. However, for a short time, the plane doesn't respond. It takes time for the air to blow over the wings before the plane appears to respond. So, it is similar when you correct your thinking. It will take a little while before your emotions catch up.

The key takeaway is this: your true value is not found in what other people think or say about you. It's not even what you think about yourself, although the right thinking will help. Your true value can be found in Jesus Christ and Him crucified. He died for your sins. The Son of God was publicly executed in the most deplorable way possible. He did it because He loves you with a great, wonderful, and intense love.

> *But God being so very rich in mercy because of His great and wonderful love with which He loved us.* (Eph 2:4)

You have an intrinsic value that's beyond measure.

Now that your self-esteem is growing, we need to guard that growth and not give back ground taken from the enemy. Three main factors can undermine your self-esteem: criticism, rejection, and the inner critic. Let's start with how to handle criticism.

## *Handling Criticism*

Do not let criticism erode your self-esteem. Your value is not found in what you have or what you've done. The first thing to realise is that criticism is merely someone's opinion. The accuracy of that opinion will vary depending on the psychological distortions that are in play with the person giving the opinion.

Then there is the question of which psychological distortions are active in you, the recipient. Are you filtering the feedback, rejecting positive comments, and accepting negative comments? It is easy to believe someone who is over-critical if that criticism aligns with an existing core belief. We'll cover core beliefs in chapter nineteen.

The way to handle criticism is to recognise that it is someone's opinion and not necessarily a fact. Then, by placing your own biases and emotions aside, assess the accuracy of that judgment. Consider how much of it is fact, and then recognize the facts as a means of improving what you do.

## *Handling Rejection*

Rejection is one of the most effective ways to erode your self-esteem, and it's a natural part of life. Your response to rejection will be heavily influenced by your current self-esteem, your core beliefs about yourself and the world, and what psychological distortions are in play.

When faced with rejection, stop and emotionally step back from the situation to observe your thought patterns. How accurate are they? Reframe the dialogue. Instead of "Why did this happen to me?" try "What might this be making possible?" Instead of "What's wrong with me?" explore "What's this teaching me?"

Scott Alan, in his book Rejection Rehab, sums up the rejection situation with one statement: "When someone says no to your idea, project, or romantic interest, they're not rejecting your worth as a person. They're making a decision based on their own needs, preferences, and circumstances." [9]

The key thing is that your value is not based on someone else's acceptance of you. Your true value is in Jesus Christ. You've picked the winning team. Don't worry about not being accepted by the popular crowd. You don't need them; they need you.

If the girl of your dreams just turned you down, you might start to entertain thoughts like: "That's it, there's no one else, I'm forever single."

How true is that statement? How likely is it that God wants you to be single? Does He not hear? Does He not see? Does He not care? Isn't it likely that God is closing the wrong door only so you can step through the right door?

The same paradigm applies to job interviews, making new friends, job promotions, and virtually any situation where rejection occurs. *You can only receive what you are given by God, and no good thing will He withhold from those who love him.* (Ps 84:11)

You may find yourself facing repeated rejection from the same individuals, establishing a pattern of ongoing rejection. This situation can be toxic, and it may be time to seek new opportunities for friendships.

After experiencing rejection, it is natural to want to withdraw. However, this reaction can be counterproductive. Instead, make an effort to stay connected with others. Remaining engaged will help build your self-confidence, which in turn will increase your resilience to rejection.

## *Inner Critic*

One last adversary to watch out for is the inner critic, which we will deal with in more detail in chapter eighteen. If he is not kept in check, he will erode your self-esteem more quickly than your outer critics.

The Bible says in Proverbs to guard your heart with all diligence, for out of it come the issues of life. Your inner critical thoughts are thoughts you need to guard your heart against. The best way to do this is by monitoring which thoughts are crossing your mind. If you find you are suddenly critical of yourself, challenge the thought. How true is this? Could I be a little too harsh on myself?

We've just covered the three most common obstacles to strong self-esteem.

## Stopping Self Doubt

> *For I can do everything through Christ who gives me strength.* (Phil 4:13)

Self-doubt is inevitable at times. We see a classic example in Judges chapter six where an angel of the Lord speaks to Gideon and sends him to fight the Midianites. There are over one hundred and thirty-five thousand Midianites. Gideon manages to gather thirty-two thousand men. God tells him there are too many. Eventually, it comes down to three hundred men. They are outnumbered four hundred and fifty to one. If anyone had justification for self-doubt, it was Gideon.

Let's start with what you are thinking. Gideon obviously needed to stand in faith. However, negative thoughts allow doubt to compromise faith. Negative thoughts don't provide a foundation for faith; positive thoughts do. Monitor and eliminate all negative thoughts while beginning to think positively. As you think, so you become. Next, start voicing positive affirmations. "*The righteous are as bold as a lion.*" (Prov 28:1) "*I can do all things through Christ who strengthens me*" (Phil 4:11) "*In all things, you are more than a conqueror.*" (Rom 8:37)

Now believe, *God is for you, so who can be against you?*

## Living Self Worth

> *For You created my inmost being; You knit me together in my mother's womb. I praise You because I am fearfully and wonderfully made.* (Psalm 139:13-14)

If you don't know your self-worth or your true value, you will seek it in someone or something that does not reflect who you are. Your true value is not based on what you have or on what others say about you. Your true value comes from Jesus Christ and Him crucified. He chose you, predestined you before the beginning of time to be adopted as a son or daughter of God. God had only one Son, Jesus. He sent Jesus to die the most shameful death for YOU. Christ died for YOU. That's the depth of the love of God for YOU.

YOU have an intrinsic value that's beyond measure.

# Who are you?

Who you think you are and who God says you are most of the time will be two different things. You will act out of what you believe about yourself. Satan wants you to think you are lower than a snake. If he can get you to think you're unworthy or you can't do it, then he has disempowered you from achieving anything for Christ.

## Who do you think you are?

When I was growing up, I told my dad I wanted to go to university and become a computer engineer. To my shock, he told me I wasn't smart enough for that. I had to leave school and get a trade, becoming a plumber or a machinist like him.

It is bad enough receiving negative input; it is even worse when it's from someone you love. I've now worked in IT for forty-five years. My Dad had it wrong. So have the people who have spoken negatively into your life.

# WHO ARE YOU?

What you think about yourself will stem from what you believe regarding people speaking into your life and how you might distort those opinions of you. My dad had an opinion of me. What he spoke out was not a fact. So it is when people speak over your life, they offer their opinion of you, which you likely didn't ask for.

In chapter five, I covered psychological distortions of the mind that stem from being inward-focused, also referred to as In-The-Box. What this does is take positive constructive criticisms and distorts them into lies. The devil doesn't have to do anything, as your mind does his work for him.

An example is filtering, where you either filter out the negative and only accept the positive, or you only accept the negative and reject the positive. Most of the time, it's the latter. The result is that your view of yourself gets lower and lower. Lower than a rattlesnake.

Another example of distortion is mind-reading. In mind-reading, you make assumptions about what someone is thinking. Imagine you are having coffee with a friend, and the conversation is warm and friendly until you mention something, and suddenly, your friend changes the subject. You immediately think you've offended her. This is the first assumption (mind-reading). From that assumption, you derive the thought that you are stupid and can't hold a conversation without offending someone.

The distortion quickly progresses to a lie.

So, how do you see yourself? Are you lower than a rattlesnake? How did you get that low? Did you get there on your own, or did Satan help?

Know this, if you think you're a low-life scumbag, that's a lie. Do you think you're ugly? Who told you that? Are you stupid? Only if you believe Satan's lies.

Lift up your eyes; the future is bright. If God is for you, who can be against you?

## Mind the Gap

There is a gap between who we think we are and who God says we are. Consider the Israelites: after four hundred years of slavery, God released them from their bondage. God sent Moses to deliver them. Similarly, He has delivered you from the bondage of sin and taken you out of the world.

The Israelites, after witnessing majestic miracles such as the parting of the sea firsthand, whinged and complained that there wasn't any food or water, and many wanted to return to slavery. Many thought God had brought them into the desert to kill them. An equally stupid thought.

They had the heart and mind of a slave.

But God had plans for His people, plans to prosper them and not to harm them. To give them a hope and a future. So has He for YOU.

God's plan was not just to deliver them from slavery but also to give them a land of their own, a land flowing with milk and honey. The promised land. However, to claim that land, they had to fight many battles, and many of those adversaries were giants almost twice their height.

Men with the heart and mind of a slave are completely unable to fight any kind of battle. When faced with the question of fight or flight, they will always choose flight.

God had to allow the generation He delivered from Egypt to die out and be replaced by a new generation that did not possess the heart and mind of a slave. These men would be the warriors capable of slaying giants.

To enter the promised land, there will be battles; there will be giants. It's time to put on the heart and mind of Christ.

## Who does God say you are?

Forget what you think and what others might think. What does God think? It's His opinion that counts.

### *You are Redeemed*

> *In him we have redemption through his blood, the forgiveness of sins, in accordance with the riches of God's grace* (Eph 1:7)

Death by crucifixion during Roman times was the worst death possible. Many scholars claim that the scourging consisted of thirty-nine lashes. That limit is what the Jews set, as many victims died after forty lashes, as the whip had metal and bone woven into it, and it used to rip the flesh from a man's back. Under Roman crucifixion, there was no limit. The process was overseen by a centurion who had one objective: don't let the prisoner die.

The Persians invented crucifixion by tying a man to a cross. But, the Romans found that by piercing the flesh of the wrist and hanging them on a cross, only in intense pain could the victim even take a breath.[10]

Only in the death on the cross is the length, the breadth, and the depth of the love of God for YOU truly revealed. You were purchased at a great price. Your true value is seen in Jesus Christ, and Him crucified.

### *You are Adopted*

> *Having predestined us to adoption as sons by Jesus Christ to Himself, according to the good pleasure of His will* (Eph 1:5)

Predestined and planned in lovingkindness before the beginning of time to be adopted, we aren't illegitimate children; instead, we have a home and a family to belong to. Whose family did we get adopted into? The God who created the Earth and all its creatures, the God who made the stars at night—over one hundred billion stars that comprise the Milky Way galaxy, which is just one of two trillion galaxies. He has adopted you because He loves you with a great, deep, and intimate love.

## *You have an Inheritance*

> *In Him also we have obtained an inheritance, being predestined according to the purpose of Him who works all things according to the counsel of His will that we who first trusted in Christ should be to the praise of His glory* (Eph 1:11)

We have been predestined to be adopted into His family. As an adopted child, you have an inheritance. You are not just redeemed, not just adopted, but riches, honour, and glory will follow you because of the price Jesus paid on the cross.

## *He Made You*

> *For You have made him a little lower than the angels,*
> *And You have crowned him with glory and honor.*
> (Psalm 8:5)

The word "Angels" in this scripture comes from the word "Elohim," which in Hebrew translates to "Gods." However, most of the time, the context for using this word refers to God in the singular, not gods plural.

Phil Pringle, in his book "Who We Are, What We Have," puts forward a strong argument that Elohim should be translated as God and not as angels. [11] If we think about this, God did not send Jesus to die for those fallen angels. There is no path of redemption for them.

If Pastor Phil is right, the scripture should read: *"For You have made him a little lower than God."* If we are adopted into His family, then it makes sense that He has made us above the angels, who are ministering spirits working for us.

## *You are a Royal Priest*

> *But you are a chosen generation, a royal priesthood, a holy nation, His own special people, that you may proclaim the praises of Him who called you out of darkness into His Marvelous light.* (1 Peter 2:9)

You were chosen to be a royal priest. Royal, as in prince or princess. But whose royal family am I talking about? The royal family of God himself. If you think being a member of the British royal family, with your own title, land, and mansion, would be cool, you're thinking too small. This is the God who, with a wave of his hand, created two trillion galaxies, each with over a billion stars, and each star with a dozen planets. Worlds without end. You are a royal member of the greatest family that ever existed.

You are the head and not the tail. You are a leader and not a follower. A leader to lead people into the full knowledge of Jesus Christ. You are blessed to be a blessing.

# Submission

God is exceedingly gracious. When we are born again, He does not expect soldiers of Christ with shiny armour. We start off a little rough, walk a little rough, talk a little rough, and as time goes by, God will talk to you about giving up certain language, certain behaviour, and stopping certain relationships with toxic friends, etc. Over time, we gradually become more like Christ. Jesus Christ is our example for how we should live our lives. This transformation also requires us to submit. The lessons of submission will happen in one of two scenarios. Either through ministry, through your job, or both.

When I was a field engineer, I was sent to a well-known TV station, to help them with an IT problem. It was amazing. The top floor was covered with red carpet, and the walls had very expensive wallpaper. Sophisticated lighting and costly ornaments adorned the area; no expense was spared. The IT department, however, was in the basement. The carpet there was threadbare, paint was flaking from the ceiling, and there weren't any windows. The room stank of mildew. Does this sound like a dungeon to you?

# SUBMISSION

I wasn't there long before the CIO (Chief Information Officer) came down from the top floor to see the IT manager. There was no "How are you guys doing?" Instead, it was, "Where's my report? It was due at 10:00am, and it's now 10:04." The IT manager replied, "Yes, sir, you will have it shortly." The CIO then took one look at me and stormed out. I do have a profound impact on people, I guess.

One of the guys leaned over to me and said, "Don't worry about him, that's just his management style."

Here, we have a work situation where the guys work in a dungeon and are subject to verbal abuse, not only submitting to a despicable individual but also going on to make excuses for him. To this day, I'm still astounded at the level of submission these guys had achieved.

It is easy to work for someone who's always nice and never asks too much of you. Bringing doughnuts in for the team for a morning tea break. I've been in IT for forty-five years, worked for numerous organizations, and found many task managers but few people managers. People managers will see the members of their team as people. Task managers see the members of their team as objects. If an object malfunctions, replace the object. Working for these kinds of people can be challenging and requires a higher level of submission. If you find yourself in this situation, know for certain that God is taking you into a higher level of submission. This will only be for a season. The challenges you face today will be gone tomorrow. There are brighter days ahead.

You will see similar scenarios in the church. People who haven't been in church long are promoted into leadership positions before they have matured as Christians. They may not have had any leadership experience. If they are leaning into God, then He will likely teach them people management skills. If they turn out to be task managers, then you know for certain that God is taking you into a greater level of submission.

## Difference of Opinion

For many years, I was involved in the 6:00 am prayer group. We were a small group of three. One day, the pastor announced that the 6:00 am prayer meeting was coming to a close. After the service, I rushed to the pastor to educate him on how important prayer was.

"Doesn't prayer underpin everything the church does?" The pastor did not offer me any explanation for his decision, nor did he have a greater plan to replace the morning meetings. When you see a manager or pastor making a choice that seems to you to be the wrong choice, you have an obligation to voice your point of view, as you might be right, and your pastor might be taking you down the wrong path. But more often than not, it's our perception that needs to change as God tests our level of submission.

## Immoral Instruction

Immoral instruction is more likely to occur in your workplace than in the church. (I hope) When you see it, you have an obligation to raise the issue with your manager. If your manager insists on continuing with this immoral instruction, then the right thing to do in this case is not to comply. Stand on your integrity. This can be a hard test of your faith.

## Moral Instruction

Let's look at some examples of submission from the bible.

In Luke 1:26 an angel of the Lord is sent to Mary with a greeting: *"Greetings, you who are highly favoured! The Lord is with you"*. Having a supernatural being appear in the room with you is a startling start to anyone's day. Then the angel continues to tell her how she will conceive and give birth to a son, who will be called Son of the Most High, and that His kingdom will never end.

Now, Mary is about fifteen years old. She's experiencing an intense supernatural event, and it's very likely in this brief dialogue that she hasn't fully comprehended everything the angel is saying.

This is her response: *"May your word to me be fulfilled."* No in-depth detail was provided. No argument with the angel, "Oh, I'm not worth it." "Can't you find someone a little older?" Mary's all in, totally on board, without knowing where this might lead. It's an example of humility, submission, and faith.

Jesus, knowing his time was near, in Luke 42:39. He goes to the Mount of Olives to pray. This is His prayer *"Father, if you are willing, take this cup from me; yet not my will, but yours be done"*. Knowing He was about to be executed in the worst way possible He asks if His father would take the cup from him, but not if it doesn't align with His Father's will.

In Luke 22:44, we read, *"And being in anguish, he prayed more earnestly, and his sweat was like drops of blood falling to the ground."* In this verse, you begin to see a depth of anguish and deep sorrow. Deep enough to cause sweats of blood. There's more going on behind the scenes than the scripture is telling us. This is before he's flogged with a device that strips the flesh from a man's back and then nailed to a cross, naked for everyone to see. Yet in all this, Jesus makes this prayer: *"Not my will, but yours be done"*.

Jesus is the example of how we should be living our lives. Totally surrendered.

# PART III

# The Way of the World

Do not conform to the pattern of this world but be transformed by the renewing of your mind. (Rom 12:2)

# World Views

Our worldview shapes the way we interpret the world around us. It answers questions like: What is real? What is a human? Is there a God? How can we know God? Is there life after death?

The list of worldviews that follows represents the most common worldviews. There are many instances where people or people groups adopt a combination of these views to synthesise a view, believing there is a little bit of truth in each of these views. This approach is also flawed as it makes an assumption that each view holds some truth, and the truth they choose to hold on to is the correct fragment of truth.

## CHRISTIAN THEISM

Christian Theism was formed with the life and death of Jesus Christ in the 1st century AD, and dominated the West up until the 1700s, forming the basis for most Christian views, including Jesuits, Anglicans & Presbyterians.[12] Each group forms a slightly different view of God. Their common view is to seek first the kingdom of God and to love God with all their heart.

## Deism

Deism holds the belief that there is a God or higher power, but that this higher power is no longer involved in the universe or human affairs. An understanding of God and oneself can be achieved through logical reasoning and observation. Autonomous reasoning replaces the Bible. This represents the first departure from Christian values.[13]

## Popular Deism

Popular Deism is an unstructured form of Deism that holds the belief in a universe created by God, who occasionally intervenes in creation. This version of Deism is simpler and can integrate existing religious beliefs with spirituality experiences.[13]

## Naturalism

God doesn't exist in this worldview, but our reasoning shapes our reality. It holds the belief that everything arises from natural causes and laws without supernatural influences.[14]

Variations of Naturalism:

- Atheism: There is no God.
- Agnosticism: We cannot know if God exists.
- Apatheism: It is not important to know whether God exists or not.

## NIHILISM

Naturalism leads to Nihilism. Nihilism, unlike all other worldviews, denies knowledge. It has no statement of values, and nothing has meaning. Knowledge cannot be trusted.

There are different types of nihilism, including:

1. Existential Nihilism – The belief that life has no inherent meaning or purpose.
2. Moral Nihilism – The idea that moral values are not objective or absolute.
3. Epistemological Nihilism – The belief that true knowledge or certainty is impossible.
4. Political Nihilism – The rejection of established social and political structures.[15]

Ethically, whatever is, is right.

## EXISTENTIALISM

Humans are free to make choices. Life has no meaning. Each individual must create their own purpose and live a life that's right in their own eyes.

There are two types of Existentialism:

- Atheistic existentialism
- Theistic existentialism

## *Atheistic Existentialism*

Atheistic existentialism is derived from naturalism. God does not exist. We can understand the universe through logical reasoning. Everything we do is right in our own eyes, as there is no moral compass.

## *Theistic Existentialism*

Theistic existentialism is derived from Theism. It combines existentialist thought with belief in God.

Like existentialism in general, it emphasizes individual existence, freedom, and choice. However, it differs from atheistic existentialism by affirming that God provides ultimate meaning and purpose.[12]

## PANTHEISM

This is the foundational worldview that underpins the Hindu Advaita Vedanta system of Shankara, the Transcendental Meditation of Maharishi Mahesh Yogi, and much of the Upanishads. Buddhism developed from Hinduism.

Pantheism is the only Eastern worldview that is monotheistic, believing in one God, which is the cosmos itself. Realising oneness with the cosmos is not a matter of belief but of technique, and even the techniques can vary. These techniques include meditation, chanting, and reciting mystical words given by a guru. However, these very techniques can lead to demonic oppression. They aim to eliminate desire and achieve salvation through union with the cosmos (Hinduism) or the void of pure consciousness (Buddhism).[12]

## New Age Movement

People who adopt the New Age Movement view the cosmos from two perspectives: the visible universe and the invisible universe. The invisible universe can be accessed through altered states of consciousness, which may arise from occult practices, meditation, psychedelic drugs, and witchcraft. However, it is not uncommon for some cults to use a combination of these practices.

New Agers seek to integrate themselves into the cosmos. There is no need for God. They are gods in their own right.[12]

## Postmodernism

Postmodernism is the reaction to modernism. It challenges ideas, narratives, and absolute truth from the perspective of objective reality. It does this by focusing on the language constructs to derive meaning.[16]

Key Features:

- Scepticism – Rejecting explanations of science, reasoning, history, and reality.
- Relativism – Argues that truth and meaning are socially constructed.
- Intertextuality – Highlights how texts, ideas, and cultural artifacts are interconnected and borrow from one another.
- Deconstruction – A method that examines how texts undermine their own meanings
- Hyperreality – Suggests that media and simulations create a reality that replaces or distorts the real world.
- Fragmentation – Challenges linear storytelling and fixed identities, favouring a mix of styles, genres, and perspectives.[17]

Ethically, good is whatever society decides is good.

## ISLAMIC THEISM

Islam believes in only one God, Allah, who is all-powerful and infinite. Muslims view death as a transition into an eternal state of either paradise or hell. Their salvation depends on closely observing the law described in the Qur'an.[18] This worldview appeals to those who seek salvation through works and the law, similar to Judaism. There is no acknowledgment of salvation by grace. Jesus Christ is regarded as a prophet but not a saviour.

## FINAL COMMENTS

You can see that world views have evolved since the 16th and 17th centuries, shifting from a Biblical worldview where we worship God, to world views that either worship false Gods or ourselves.

For those wanting to know more about worldviews, I'd highly recommend a book called The Universe Next Door by James W. Sire.[12]

# Influence of Media

The devil uses media to influence the thinking of the masses. Movies, news channels, gaming (just to name a few), and the internet provide platforms that are filled with misinformation, opinions, and biased, distorted views of the facts. Let's start with movies.

## Movies

We often view movies as a way to pass the time, but we seldom reflect on the power this medium has to shape our feelings, thoughts, and actions. Our identification with the actor in the film greatly influences our thoughts and feelings. This is especially evident in teenagers who are still forming their identity.

Watching violent movies can desensitize viewers to violence and increase aggressive behaviour, especially in children and adolescents. It promotes the idea that violence is normal. Glamorizing substance abuse in a film increases the likelihood of the viewer turning to smoking or drinking.

Promoting sexual promiscuity increases the chances of the viewer engaging in sex outside of marriage.

Additionally, Hollywood has made a concerted effort to normalize witchcraft and occult practices with the presentation of nice witches and people who use their occult powers to do good. At the same time, Hollywood is promoting homosexuality with gay themes showing up in just about every second film you watch.

Horror and pornographic films have a spiritual influence, opening the door to either a spirit of fear or a spirit of lust. Both of these can derail your Christian walk. As a young Christian, I watched numerous horror films, thinking they were a joke. Many are, but one night I dreamed I was watching a horror film and something leaped off the screen and attacked me. These types of films are not a joke, and there are consequences for watching them. Similarly, you might watch a film with a pornographic scene and think it's a one-off, and that we're all good. You could be deceiving yourself. Remember this: a small deviation in the way, over time, leads to a large deviation in the way.[4] Don't give the devil a foothold. Uproot the weed before the roots get established.

Not all movies are necessarily bad for you. Watching sad films can produce an emotional release, which has physical benefits and promotes good mental health. Documentaries can be informative, offering a new perspective on a topic. Some fictional stories can stir up empathy in an area such as homosexuality, which was previously taboo. [19]

## News Channels

Mainstream news channels and fake news channels exist. The important thing to realise is that mainstream news channels sometimes get it wrong. They can present biased reports. Some news items are actually paid for to promote a product. Other news items exist to tarnish someone's reputation. Some news items consist of opinions disguised as news, advocating the author's point of view. For more information, see chapter eleven, Misinformation.

Fake news channels often present news items based on certain facts to provide a sense of credibility. These facts are then distorted, and you may not realize how distorted they are until you conduct your own fact-finding mission.

## Gaming

Playing a video game that offers a reward for beating an opponent or reaching the highest score triggers dopamine, inducing a feeling of pleasure. The game becomes addictive as you seek that pleasure hit.

Excessive gaming leads to relationship issues, sleep disturbances, and mental and physical health problems. People addicted to gaming often have low self-esteem, display impulsive and aggressive behaviour, and suffer from anxiety and depression.[20] The question to ask yourself is, "Do I control the game or does it control me?" "Is it a foothold or a stronghold?"

As with movies, action and combat games that promote violence can negatively impact you. Horror games are also not beneficial for your Christian walk.

Not all gaming is bad. Gaming in moderation can be beneficial for mental health by improving mood and focus while also providing stress relief. With online gaming and the inclusion of chat rooms, you can make friends and form connections. However, be warned that these chat rooms are sometimes exploited to groom and radicalise young marginalised individuals into extremist groups.

## Bloggers

Bloggers on social media can write and promote anything they want without being accountable to anyone. And they do. Many are paid to promote products, and they are influencers. Others do it because they have a following that boosts their ego, not because they are knowledgeable on the subject.

A great example of this is bloggers offering stock market investment advice. Most of these individuals are traders who have lost money, so they turn to a blog service you pay for. They no longer trade or purchase the recommended shares because they are losers; they lost their investments, and if you follow them, you will lose too.

# Influence of Social Media

We all need to be connected. God did not make us to live in isolation. People who are well-connected are mentally healthy, happier, and joyful, and live fulfilling lives. People living isolated lives often suffer a variety of mental health issues, including loneliness, anxiety, and depression.

## IMPACT OF SOCIAL MEDIA

Social media, to some extent, helps people stay connected. However, it's no substitute for face-to-face communication. Albert Mehrabian, a well-known expert on body language, discovered that communication consists of fifty-five percent body language, thirty-eight percent vocal (tone, etc.), and only seven percent words.[21] Some social media platforms provide the vocal elements and words, but you lose the body language.

Social media doesn't give you the same rich experience as a face-to-face connection. There is no handshake, intimate hug, or form of touch whatsoever. There's a certain warmth that only comes from a face-to-face connection.

Social media is no substitute for face-to-face reality.

Social media does have some benefits:

- Communicate with family and friends
- Make new friends
- Join or promote worthwhile causes
- Seek or offer support to those in need
- Find social and professional connections
- Express yourself creatively
- Access valuable learning material

Social media does have some problems:

- Inadequacy concerning your life or appearance
- Fear of missing out
- Isolation
- Depression and anxiety
- Cyberbullying
- Self-absorption

Let's look at those problems in more detail.

## *Inadequacy about your appearance*

Feeling inadequate about your appearance is driven by envy and dissatisfaction when seeing posts and photos of friends lying on the beach in the warmth, wearing just a bikini. No stress, just sunning themselves for that perfect tan. You may not realise the photos have been airbrushed and manipulated to look better than they are. Nevertheless, you can't live up to that kind of image. This problem has its basis in comparing yourself with someone with an unrealistic lifestyle.

## *Fear of Missing Out*

Fear of Missing Out, otherwise known as FOMO, creates the compulsion to pick up the phone and check for posts, which is almost a form of addiction. Research has proven this to be one of the main sources of social media addiction.

## *Isolation*

University research has revealed that social media platforms increase feelings of isolation and loneliness.

## *Depression and Anxiety*

Depression and anxiety stem from a lack of face-to-face connection. In-person conversations can elevate your emotions much more effectively than any social media interaction.

## *Cyberbullying*

Cyberbullying is reported by about ten percent of teens. How many more are not reporting it?

Platforms like Instagram, Facebook, TikTok, and YouTube use machine learning to detect abusive or harmful content automatically. However, the accuracy of the AI models detecting cyberbullying can be inaccurate, blocking good content and letting abusive content through.

The best solution to cyberbullying currently is to block or mute the offender.

## *Self-absorption*

Self-absorption is derived from an unhealthy, self-centred focus on posting countless selfies and personal thoughts. These selfies and personal thoughts are then weaponised by cyber bullies.

## SOCIAL MEDIA ADDICTION

Whenever you receive a like or positive reaction to something you've posted, it triggers the release of dopamine in the brain, providing you with feelings of pleasure, satisfaction, and motivation—a kind of reward. The more you are rewarded, the more time you spend on social media. It's an addiction to instant gratification.

To reinforce this addiction, we have FOMO, Fear Of Missing Out. There isn't any post or any response to your posts that can't wait until tomorrow. Yet, we sleep with our phones next to our beds, waiting for a ping that indicates a response that we feel compelled to reply to in the middle of the night. We are seeking instant gratification, and a lack of sleep leads to other problems.

Your social media addiction can be driven by other factors such as stress, depression, and boredom. Do you turn to social media only when feeling down? Social media might be compensating for other problems.

We'll next have a look at the cycle that reinforces this social media addiction.

## Cycle of Social Media[22]

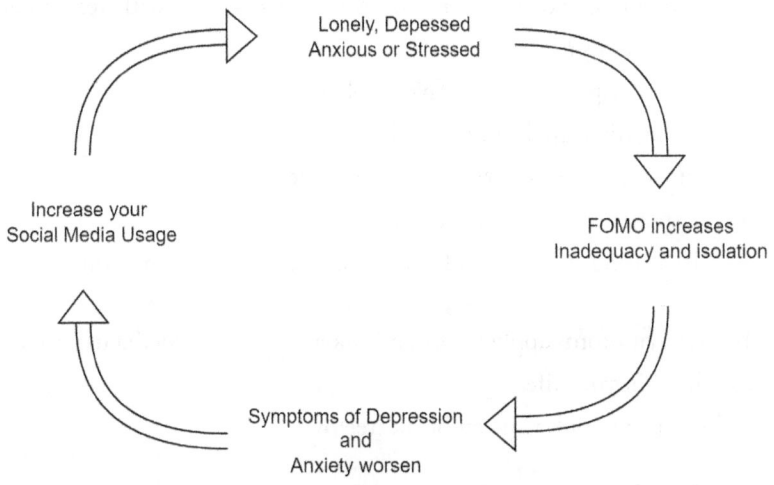

Figure 10.1 – The Cycle of Social Media

This cycle begins with feelings of anxiety, depression, and/or stress. To seek relief, you turn to social media. As FOMO increases, so do feelings of inadequacy and isolation. These negative emotions exacerbate your symptoms, leading you to increase your social media usage. Thus, the cycle continues.

Breaking FOMO is the key to breaking this unhealthy cycle. Fear Of Missing Out is just a fear and an unfounded fear. It is built on the precept of instant gratification. Spiritual maturity comes from accepting delayed gratification instead. Is delayed gratification any less gratifying? Will the likes mean anything less tomorrow? [22]

## Signs of a Social Media Stronghold

Symptoms to observe:
- Do you spend more time on social media than with real friends face-to-face?
- Comparing yourself unfavourably to others
- Being distracted from school or work
- Putting yourself at risk just to gain likes
- Experiencing sleep degradation
- Increasing symptoms of anxiety, depression, and isolation

If these symptoms apply to you, it is likely that social media has become a stronghold in your life.

If it's a stronghold, you can break free by:

- Limiting your online time
- Turning off your phone at night
- Not bringing your phone to the dining table
- Setting specific times during the day to check your posts
- Avoiding social media to overcome boredom; find something else to focus on during these times.
- Before you post anything, ask yourself: Is it true? Is it right? Is it necessary? And what does it achieve? Hopefully, you won't post anything you will regret later. (Prov 8:12 Wisdom dwells with prudence.

If you can't break the stronghold through self-control, then ask God prayerfully for help and to strengthen you. It is also possible that the stronghold has progressed to bondage, in which case you need to seek help from a Christian counsellor.

## INFLUENCE OF SOCIAL MEDIA

Social media, in small amounts, can be very helpful for staying connected. But too much has adverse consequences. Do you control your social media usage, or does it control you?

# Peer Pressure

Peer pressure is the pressure to conform to what others are doing or saying. This essentially means you are controlled by what other people might think or say.[23]

*A righteous man who falters before the wicked Is like a murky spring and a polluted well.* (Prov 25:26)

## KEY FACTORS OF PEER PRESSURE

Peer pressure is a psychological phenomenon in which individuals are influenced by their peers to adopt certain behaviours, attitudes, or values. It can be both positive and negative, depending on the context.

The psychology behind peer pressure is driven by several key factors:

1. **The Need to Belong (Social Identity Theory)**

    Humans have an innate need to belong to social groups. According to Social Identity Theory, people derive a sense of self-esteem from group membership. When a person's identity is tied to a group, they may conform to the group's norms to maintain acceptance and avoid rejection.

2. **Fear of Rejection (Social Conformity)**

    People often conform to peer pressure out of fear of rejection or exclusion. Studies, such as Solomon Asch's conformity experiments, show that individuals may go along with the majority even when they know it's wrong, simply to avoid standing out.

3. **The Influence of Authority and Role Models**

    Peers viewed as leaders or high-status individuals within a group exert greater pressure. Social Learning Theory (Bandura) suggests that people model their behaviours after those they admire, increasing the likelihood of adopting their actions.

4. **Cognitive Dissonance**

    When someone's personal beliefs conflict with group behaviour, they may experience cognitive dissonance (mental discomfort). To reduce this discomfort, they might change their behaviour or beliefs to align with the group.

5. **Reward and Punishment (Operant Conditioning)**

    Peer pressure operates through reinforcement mechanisms:
    - **Positive reinforcement**: Approval, praise, or inclusion when conforming.
    - **Negative reinforcement**: Avoiding ridicule, criticism, or exclusion by following the group.

6. **The Impact of Social Media**
    Modern peer pressure extends beyond face-to-face interactions. Social comparison theory suggests that people evaluate themselves based on others, and social media amplifies this effect by constantly exposing individuals to peer behaviours and expectations.
7. **Developmental Factors**
    - **Adolescents** are more susceptible to peer pressure due to ongoing brain development, particularly in the prefrontal cortex (responsible for decision-making) and the limbic system (which drives emotions and rewards).
    - **Adults** experience peer pressure too, but it often manifests in workplace culture, lifestyle choices, or social norms.[24]

## TYPES OF PEER PRESSURE

Types of Peer Pressure you will experience:
1. **Direct Peer Pressure** – When someone explicitly tells or pressures you to do something (e.g., a friend pushing you to drink at a party).
2. **Indirect Peer Pressure** is when you feel the need to conform based on what others around you are doing (e.g., dressing a certain way to fit in).
3. **Positive Peer Pressure** – Encouragement to adopt good habits, such as studying harder or exercising.
4. **Negative Peer Pressure** – Influence to engage in harmful or risky behaviours, like smoking, excessive spending, drinking too much, or unethical actions.
5. **Unspoken Peer Pressure** – When social norms influence behaviour, even if no one directly pressures you (e.g., feeling the need to upgrade your lifestyle to match colleagues).[25]

## INFLUENCE OF PEER PRESSURE

The spiritual impact of peer pressure can be profound, influencing a person's beliefs, values, and overall sense of self. It can either strengthen or weaken your journey, depending on whether the pressure aligns with or contradicts your inner values.

Here are some key ways peer pressure can affect your spirituality:

1. **Strengthening or Weakening Faith**
   - Being surrounded by spiritually uplifting Christians can encourage deeper faith, greater discipline, and moral growth.
   - Pressure to conform to behaviours that contradict your beliefs can create spiritual confusion, guilt, or even a loss of faith over time.
2. **Conflict Between Inner Convictions and External Expectations**
   - When pressured to act against your values, it can create internal struggles, leading to anxiety, guilt, or a sense of spiritual disconnect.
   - Constantly seeking approval from others may weaken personal discernment and reliance on Christian guidance.
3. **Growth Through Challenge**
   - Resisting negative peer pressure can strengthen resilience, deepen self-awareness, and reinforce commitment to your walk in Christ.
   - Facing opposition to your faith can lead to personal transformation and a stronger sense of identity.
4. **Impact on Purpose and Direction**
   - Positive peer support can inspire someone to pursue a more meaningful, purpose-driven life.

- Negative influences may cause you to drift away from your walk in Christ, leading to feelings of emptiness or a lack of fulfilment.
5. **Influence on Mindset**
    - Surrounding oneself with spiritually uplifting peers can raise one's morale, promoting peace and growth.
    - Negative peer environments can drain your morale, fostering negativity, doubt, or a sense of spiritual stagnation.

Ultimately, the spiritual impact of peer pressure depends on how you respond to it. Developing a strong sense of self-worth, seeking supportive relationships, and staying connected to spirit-filled believers can help maintain inner peace, authenticity, and a relationship with Christ. [23]

## SITUATIONS OF PEER PRESSURE

Peer pressure can occur in a variety of situations, influencing people in both positive and negative ways. Here are some common scenarios where peer pressure might occur:

1. **School and Academics**
    - Friends encouraging you to skip class or cheat on a test.
    - Pressure to take certain subjects or perform at a certain level.
    - Feeling the need to participate in extracurricular activities just because others are doing it.
2. **Social Situations**
    - Being pressured to drink alcohol, smoke, or try drugs at a party.
    - Feeling the need to dress a certain way to fit in.
    - Joining in on gossip or bullying to be accepted by a group.

3. **Workplace and Career**
   - Co-workers pushing you to stay late even if you don't want to.
   - Feeling pressure to follow unethical practices to get ahead.
   - Being influenced to act more competitively or aggressively than you normally would.
4. **Family Expectations**
   - Pressure to pursue a specific career because it's a family tradition.
   - Expecting to marry or have kids before you are ready to because of family norms.
   - Feeling the need to conform to religious or cultural expectations.
5. **Sports and Hobbies**
   - Teammates pushing you to play through an injury.
   - Feeling pressured to train harder or take performance-enhancing drugs.
   - Being encouraged to engage in dangerous stunts or extreme activities.
6. **Online and Social Media**
   - Feeling pressured to follow trends, post in a certain way, or edit photos.
   - Joining in on online challenges that might be risky or dangerous.
   - Feeling the need to compare yourself to influencers or celebrities.
7. **Relationships and Dating**
   - Pressure to enter a relationship before you're ready.
   - Being encouraged to act a certain way to impress a partner.

- Feeling the need to stay in a toxic relationship because of social expectations.
8. **Consumer and Financial Decisions**
    - Pressure to buy expensive brands or keep up with the spending habits of friends.
    - Feeling the need to go out frequently, even when you want to save money.
    - Being encouraged to invest in trends like cryptocurrency or NFTs, without proper knowledge.[26]

Peer pressure can be direct, with someone explicitly telling you to do something, and indirect, with you feeling like you should do something because others are doing it. It's important to recognise these influences and make choices that align with your values.

## STOPPING PEER PRESSURE

We all need to be liked, appreciated, and respected. When people are love-starved, they look to others to fill the void and behave in ways to earn that love and acceptance. Usually out of fear of losing that source of love. Understanding the love of God overcomes this need. [23]

To overcome peer pressure, there's a spiritual journey you need to take, moving away from the fear of man, no longer considering what someone might think or say, and towards what God thinks and says about YOU. Through meditating on the Word of God, you can gain revelation and knowledge of the love of Christ for YOU. The length, the breadth, and the depth of the Love of Christ for YOU, which passes all understanding.

This is knowledge that is beyond knowing. You can't catch it in your head; you can only catch it in your heart. It is this revelatory knowledge that will reveal your true value and self-worth. When you understand how God sees you and values you, you won't need anyone else's approval.

The devil does not want you to know who you are in Christ. Knowing your true worth and the love of Christ for you not only eliminates the need to seek love and acceptance from your peers but also fills you with genuine love for those peers.

Without the need for love and acceptance from peers, there is no basis for fear of man. Without fear of man, you will find love for man, and in that place, you are in a position to reach out to the lost.

## SCRIPTURES TO MEDITATE ON

> *But you are a chosen generation, a royal priesthood, a holy nation, His own people, that you may proclaim the praises of Him who called you out of darkness into His Marvelous light.*
> (1 Peter 2:9)

You are not only chosen, redeemed from destruction by the blood of Christ, but chosen to be a royal priest.

> *"The Lord your God is with you, the Mighty Warrior who saves. He will take great delight in you; in his love he will no longer rebuke you, but will rejoice over you with singing."*
> (Zep 3:17)

He, God Almighty, takes great delight in YOU. He rejoices over YOU with singing. How great is that love for YOU?

> *He chose us in him before the foundation of the world, that we should be holy and without blame before him, In love hav-*

*ing predestined us for adoption as sons by Jesus Christ, according to the purpose of his will.* (Eph 1:3)

YOU have been chosen before the beginning of time, predestined according to God's loving plan for YOU, to be adopted into His family. He chose YOU; you didn't choose Him. To be redeemed from destruction, YOU aren't redeemed to be an illegitimate child but an adopted child. Adopted into a Royal Family. O, thanks be to Jesus in whom we triumph.

# Misinformation

Information about the world we live in has increased dramatically over the last fifty years. Mostly, thanks for scientific discoveries at all levels of science. Thanks to the internet, this information is easily dispersed, and everyone can be kept well-informed all the time. While it is easy to fall victim to information overload, being informed is generally a good thing.

However, the internet is a tool, and like most tools, it can be used for both evil and good. When information is twisted and distorted before being propagated, it becomes difficult to distinguish truth from lies and facts from fiction.

In this chapter, we will look at how misinformation impacts our view and understanding of the world we live in.

## SCIENCE AS A SOURCE OF TRUTH

Scientists, when reviewing the results of tests, will sometimes have a biased view. They may have a political agenda and be looking for or expecting a certain outcome. They may have preconceived ideas on what to expect or think they know the outcome, and barely consider the test result findings. They can also be influenced by whatever society they belong to, not wanting to fall out with anyone else's point of view. Some scientists ignore results that conflict with the outcome they are biased towards. They make conclusions without having all the facts, simply to wrap up an investigation and move on.[27]

Not so long ago, people believed the Earth was flat and that the stars at night moved across the sky. Then, science changed its view and discovered that the Earth was round. Later, they found that some of those stars were other planets similar to Earth. However, they still held on to the belief that the Earth was the centre of everything. Finally, the view emerged that those points of light were, in fact, other suns that were part of a larger structure called a galaxy. The Earth wasn't the centre of anything.

Many of our scientific worldviews today have been formed without knowing all the facts. But, as science matures, it reveals more and more the glory and majesty of the God who created it. As science matures, it only reaffirms the Bible; it doesn't discredit it.

> *For since the creation of the world His invisible attributes are clearly seen, being understood by the things that are made, even His eternal power and Godhead, so that they are without excuse.* (Rom 1:20)

## Conformity and Consensus

In a social media setting, misinformation can spread like wildfire. One way this happens is through conformity within the group.

MISINFORMATION

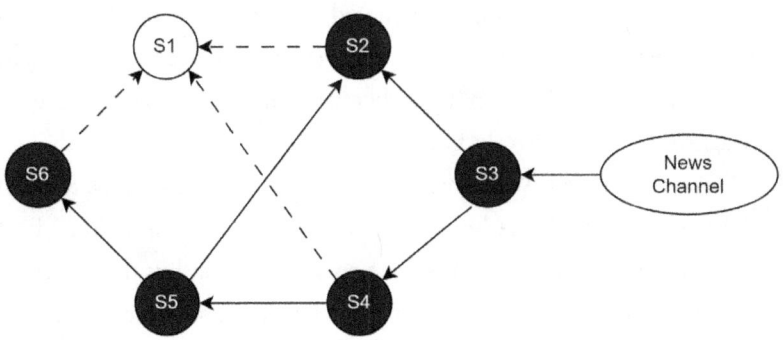

Figure 12.1 – Misinformation Propagation

In this diagram, S3 receives a news report and shares it with S2 and S4, who believe the report. Both S2 and S4 share the report with S1, who does not believe it. In this situation, S1 is under pressure to conform his or her beliefs to align with those of the group, regardless of the truth.

What if there was a distinct lack of conformity?

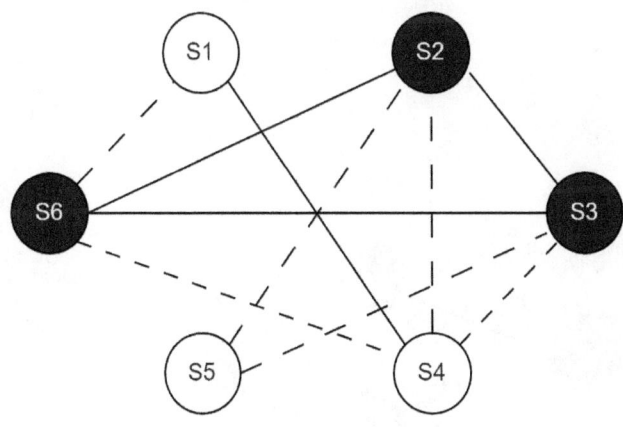

Figure 12.2 – Lack of Conformity

In this diagram, individuals represented by black circles reached conclusion A, while those represented by white circles reached conclusion B. This created a sense of distrust among individuals represented by dotted lines. This distrust exists on two levels: the data the others possess and the way that data is interpreted. While distrust exists, no consensus can be reached.

What if you replace the individuals with church denominations? Each starts with the same data, the Bible as a source of truth, but they interpret that truth differently. Some denominations believe signs and miracles were only for the first-century church. Other denominations think that praying in tongues is demonic. While distrust exists between groups, there can never be a consensus and unity that the church is supposed to represent. [27]

## Trusted Sources

Trust has a lot to do with whom we accept information from. Scientists, pastors, and the government are supposed to be trusted sources of information.

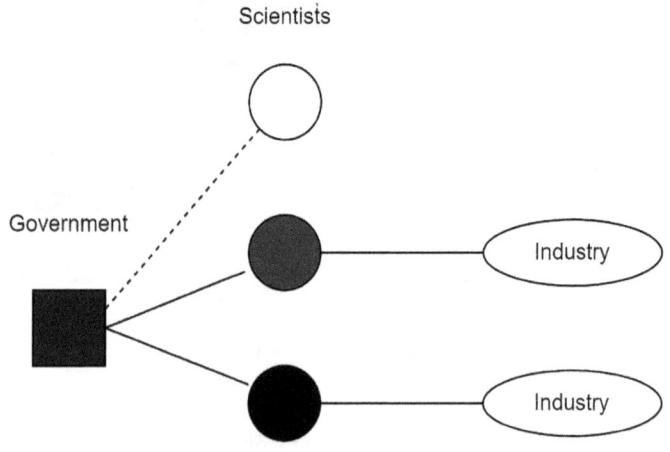

Figure 12.3 – Industries influence Scientists and Government

Scientists can be manipulated by industry to ensure that governments do not create policies that negatively impact their industry. Industries with environmental impacts are an example of this.

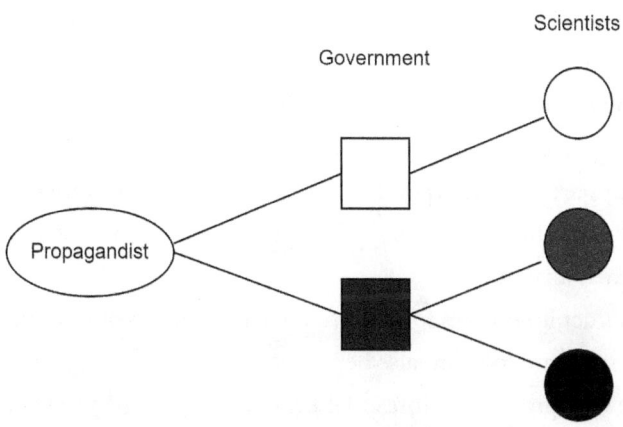

Figure 12.4 – Government influenced by Propagandists

Propagandists will also lobby the government to make or change policies that conform to their agenda.[27]

Be aware that trusted sources are going to get it wrong from time to time.

## Fake News

Journalists who report the news are always searching for stories that can boost their sales and media presence. They seek out stories that are sensational or have the potential to become sensational. For instance, if they turn to scientists for a story and receive conflicting views, they will often favour the view that is more sensational, even if it later proves to be false. Some reputable news channels, such as Fox, CNN, and MSNBC, will apologize for getting it wrong once the true facts are revealed. However, most news channels will not admit when they are wrong.

The news you see is driven by journalists who aim to write sensational articles that will capture the broadest audience possible and boost their media ratings. Therefore, if a news item is true, it is likely sensationalized. If the journalist has any bias, whether stemming from personal beliefs or the perspective of their employer, that bias will obscure the facts that do not support their viewpoint.[27] When truly engaging stories are scarce, news channels often fill the void with opinions dressed as news, sometimes referred to as analysis.

The harder it becomes for us to find reliable sources of information, the more likely we are to form false beliefs.

These newsgroups can spread falsehoods, making the problem of finding true news much more difficult. It is not as simple as pointing to reliable and unreliable sources, since a lot of news channels are considered reliable.

A more dangerous version of misinformation is conspiracy theories

## Conspiracy Theories

If you take the numeric value of the letters that make up the word "Apple," it adds up to the number 666. What fruit led Adam astray? An apple. Apple Inc. has one intention: world dominance and control.

I recently shared this theory with a friend as a joke, but to my amazement, he didn't laugh. Instead, he replied, "I'm not surprised, the kids of today are brainwashed into believing they need an iPhone and not just any iPhone but the latest iPhone." My friend wasn't a stupid guy; he was well-respected businessman.

I guarantee that if you take this statement and post it somewhere on the internet, then there will be a group of people who will believe it, and you will have the beginning of a conspiracy theory.

I have identified several reasons why conspiracy theories can be appealing:

1. Seeking control and order
2. Confirmation bias
3. Erosion of trust
4. Cognitive biases
5. Emotional drivers
6. The need for belonging
7. Desire for uniqueness[28]

Misinformation exploits our emotions through sensational headlines, inflammatory language, and appeals to fear and anger. When you see this occur, take a step back and analyse the information objectively.

## MISINFORMATION AND THE BIBLE

Consider a visiting speaker who comes to church. His source of truth is the Bible, the Holy Word of God that does not change.

Believer ← Visiting Speaker (The Filtered Word of God) ← Bible (Source of Truth)

*Figure 12.5 – Distorting the Word of God*

He will teach out of his interpretation of the Word of God.

Consider this verse:

> *The God who made the world and everything in it, being Lord of heaven and earth, does not live in temples made by man,* **nor is he served by human hands**, *as though he needed anything since he himself gives to all mankind life and breath and everything.* (Act 17:24)

"Nor is He served by human hands." From this, you can gather that we are not meant to clap in church, as that does not give service to God. You could also conclude that God doesn't need your service, period. However, when you read the whole chapter in context, you quickly see that Paul is addressing the practice of idol-making, not the practice of worshipping the living God.

How about this:

> *But every woman who prays or prophesies with her head uncovered dishonours her head, for that is one and the same as if her head were shaved* (1 Cor 11:6)

From this, you can gather that all women in the church should have their heads covered. To not cover her head is shameful.

To get to the truth of this, we need to consider the culture of the time. Most women in the first century did cover their heads, but there was a division between the upper and lower classes, where the upper class wanted to show off their hairstyles.[29] Paul, in his letter, is addressing a cultural issue that is specific to the first-century church. To create a theological doctrine around this is misleading.

What if the information could not be twisted but is denied?

> Now a man who was lame from birth was being carried to the temple gate called Beautiful, where he was put every day to beg from those going into the temple courts. When he saw Peter and John about to enter, he asked them for money. Peter looked straight at him, as did John. Then Peter said, "Look at us!" So the man gave them his attention, expecting to get something from them. Then Peter said, "Silver or gold I do not have, but what I do have I give you. In the name of Jesus Christ of Nazareth, walk." Taking him by the right hand, he helped him up, and instantly the man's feet and ankles became strong. He jumped to his feet and began to walk. Then he went with them into the temple courts, walking and jumping, and praising God (Act 3:1-8)

Many theologians claim that these signs and wonders were only for the first-century church. There is no scriptural context that supports or denies this. However, there is overwhelming evidence that people are miraculously healed and set free in the church today. These theologians then attempt to justify their view and insist that these miraculous healings are the work of the devil.

> A good tree cannot bear bad fruit, and a bad tree cannot bear good fruit (Matt 7:18)

The bad fruit is not the supernatural healings seen in the church today; the bad fruit is what comes from speakers and teachers who distort the

Bible. In each of these cases, there is nothing wrong with the source of information (The Bible). It is the source of all truth. However, our interpretation of it can become distorted when viewed out of context.

## Final Comments

Lack of communication is a foothold for misinformation and demonic influence, just as much as twisted information. Satan attacks marriages to divide and conquer. A lack of communication between couples serves as an avenue for the devil. This same principle applies to most relationships and particularly those within the church.

# Discernment

The answer to misinformation is discernment. Discernment is much more than just discerning if a prophecy is from God or the devil. With the increase in misinformation, finding the truth is becoming increasingly difficult. Every time you listen to a news article, read a book, or listen to a preacher's message, you will need discernment. Even your most trusted source of information will get it wrong from time to time.

> *Do not despise prophecies but **test everything*** (Thes 5:20-21)

Discernment is closely related to wisdom. It involves judging whether something is true or false, and that judgment can only be made accurately through the eyes of wisdom.

> *A wise man's heart discerns both time and judgement, because for every matter there is a time and judgement* (Eccl 8:5-6)

There are three levels of discernment:

1. Physical Discernment – discerning someone's attitude from their body language
2. Intellectual Discernment – intellectually judging if something aligns with the Word of God.
3. Spiritual Discernment – relies on our spiritual six senses to get a knowing that something is not from God.

## Physical Discernment

Physical discernment involves reading body language. Communication consists of only seven percent words, thirty-eight percent tone, and fifty-five percent body language.[21] If their body language says one thing and they verbally say something else, then they are lying. The subject of body language is beyond the scope of this book; however, if you want to dive into this in-depth, I recommend "The Definitive Book of Body Language" by Allan and Barbara Please.

Some examples of postures to look for:

- A sudden crossing of arms while you are trying to explain something. This communicates that they have lost interest and have their own opinion.
- A sudden clasping of hands behind their head while tilting their head back. This communicates that they believe they know the answer, and you don't. Arrogance has risen up.

A useful exercise is to engage in a conversation with a non-believer and suddenly mention church or Christ. Does their body language change? Do they seem uncomfortable? Are they more or less open to this conversation?

The body language and tone of their language will give you clues to the spirit of the man or woman.

## Intellectual Discernment

Intellectual discernment can also be achieved when all the facts are present and both sides of a story are known. It involves seeking points of difference and deciding which path is true and which is false.

However, when misinformation is applied, you only get the bias of the reported news, or the story is sensationalised, and then all the facts are not known. People make decisions based on the knowledge they have. This leads to division, as you see in the US with Donald Trump.

When it comes to theology and scripture, we must turn to the Bible as the source of truth with which to measure. Does the sermon line up with our knowledge of the word? Did the speaker go off track and introduce his own speculative idea? Could there be any truth in that idea?

Another paradigm is our own thinking. Logical and rational thinking consists of a chain of related thoughts and ideas. The devil can inject thoughts into your mind that appear as unrelated ideas.

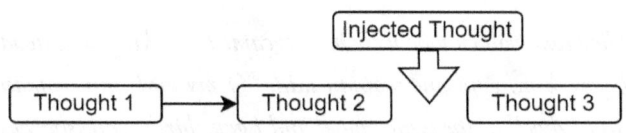

Figure 13.1 – Thought Train

The Holy Spirit can also talk to you this way. Much intellectual discernment can be gained by asking the question, "What does it achieve?" You will know right from wrong by observing the fruit that it produces. The fruit may not be obvious at first, but when you notice bad fruit starting to develop, you know to back off.

## Spiritual Discernment

Spiritual discernment is knowing that you know something is right or something is wrong. If a well-known prophet in the church prophesies a word from God and then adds his or her stuff to it as an amendment, it is difficult to know when God stopped and the prophet started in the flesh. This takes a higher level of discernment, spiritual discernment.

*Beloved do not believe every spirit, but test the spirits to see whether they are from God, for many false prophets have gone out into the world* (1 John 4:1)

There are times when you want to believe something is true, and your bias toward the situation blocks you from realising that spiritual discernment is, in fact, the opposite.

If you sense something is wrong in the spiritual atmosphere, you need to ask, "Why do I feel that way?" Ask God to reveal what's really going on.

A classic example of spiritual discernment is found in 1 Kings 3:16-28

*Now two women who were harlots came to the king, and stood before him. And one woman said, "O my lord, this woman and I dwell in the same house; and I gave birth while she was in the house. Then it happened, the third day after I had given birth, that this woman also gave birth. And we were together; no one was with us in the house, except the two of us in the house. And this woman's son died in the night, because she lay on him. So she arose in the middle of the night and took my*

> son from my side, while your maidservant slept, and laid him in her bosom, and laid her dead child in my bosom. And when I rose in the morning to nurse my son, there he was, dead. But when I had examined him in the morning, indeed, he was not my son whom I had borne." Then the other woman said, "No! But the living one is my son, and the dead one is your son." And the first woman said, "No! But the dead one is your son, and the living one is my son." Thus they spoke before the king.
>
> And the king said, "The one says, 'This is my son, who lives, and your son is the dead one'; and the other says, 'No! But your son is the dead one, and my son is the living one.'

Consider the situation presented to King Solomon. Based on the information provided, it is not possible to intellectually discern who is the rightful mother. Let's read on.

> Then the king said, "Bring me a sword." So they brought a sword before the king. And the king said, "Divide the living child in two, and give half to one, and half to the other." Then the woman whose son was living spoke to the king, for she yearned with compassion for her son; and she said, "O my lord, give her the living child, and by no means kill him!". But the other said, "Let him be neither mine nor yours, but divide him." So the king answered and said, "Give the first woman the living child, and by no means kill him; she is his mother."

To the intellectual mind, the idea of dividing the child and giving each of them half is absurd. But this was the one statement that would reveal the true nature of both women: one yearning to save her child, and the other unwilling to let either of them have him. Wisdom and understanding underpin discernment, and when it comes to spiritual discernment, the more wisdom, the better.

This type of discernment can only be reached with a close relationship with God. The closer you get to the Son, the better you can see.

## Discernment Of Dreams

Dreams tend to be highly symbolic in nature. They can relate to you, someone you know, your family, the church, or the nation. They may originate from God, the devil, or yourself. Most dreams arise from the self and feature symbolic imagery connected to your current circumstances, desires, and aspirations. If you wake up feeling unsettled by the dream, it is likely from either God or the devil.

Write the dream down. Ask yourself what the symbols mean to you. Are the symbols described in the Bible? What is the overall theme of the dream? What emotion does the dream communicate? Who is the main character? There are several books I can recommend to help in understanding the symbolic imagery. Dream Language by James Goll [30] and The Divinity Code: The Keys to Decoding Your Dreams and Visions by Adam Thompson. [31]

Can I suggest that you don't immediately act on your dream? Just because a dream communicates a blessing, don't assume it is from God. Ask God to confirm the dream in His word. When I've done this, God has spoken to me in my quiet time with Him. When I haven't done this, it has led to disaster.

## Exercises

The following exercises are designed to help sharpen your discernment in various ways. As you practice, you will find that your ability to discern begins to flow as a natural gift. When you receive words from previously trusted individuals, you will find yourself mentally challenging their point of view. When this happens, don't immediately contest their perspective, even if you believe they are mistaken. Present your enlightened view as a "What if" so as not to assert that they are wrong and you have discerned correctly. In this way, you will get to keep your friend.

## *Prophecy*

Select a Prophecy that has been spoken over you. Use your newfound discernment to discern if this was from God or in the Flesh.

## *Dream*

Select a dream you recently had. Is the dream connected to your current circumstances, or might it pertain to a future time? Is it from God, the devil, or perhaps just your own wishful thinking?

## *News Report*

Open your browser to https://www.cnn.com/ and select a news story. What can you discern about this story? Has it been exaggerated? Are all the facts presented? Have the facts been distorted? Has it been written with a biased view? Does the author use the article to promote their agenda?

## *A Prophetic Word*

Hop on your computer and open your browser to https://fathersheart-ministry.net/category/daily-prophetic-word/, then choose a prophecy. Does the prophecy contradict the word of God? Does it seem to be written in the Spirit of God? What's your gut feeling? Not your emotional feelings, but your spiritual feelings. This exercise will help you discern between your emotions and the gentle tugging of the Holy Spirit.

## *A Conspiracy Theory*

Open your browser to https://gizadeathstar.com/ and choose a conspiracy. Can you identify any facts about the story? Has the author started with facts and, at some point, distorted them into something false? If so, at what point did fact transform into fiction? Could the entire story be true? Could the entire story be a lie?

## *A Blog*

Open your browser to https://www.huffpost.com/ and choose a blog to read. Can you identify any facts about the story? Has the author started with facts and, at some point, twisted the facts into something false? If so, at what point did fact become fiction? Could the entire story be true?

## *A Book*

Find a secular non-fiction book to test your discernment. Examine the table of contents. Does the subject matter align with the book's focus? Choose and read one chapter at random. What can you discern about the author? Does he or she possess high moral values? Does he or she address the subject well? Does the author use many words to convey little? Can you discern whether the book presents fact, fantasy, or both?

## *Youtube*

Open your browser to https://www.youtube.com/ and search for presentations on spiritual warfare. View just one. What can you discern from the presentation? Is what is being presented aligned with the word of God? Is the presenter making unfounded speculations? If so, where do the facts

# DISCERNMENT

stop and fiction begin? Do you discern what is being presented in the spirit of God? What is your gut feeling telling you?

I should warn you that there are a lot of wacky YouTube teachings on Spiritual warfare. There are also a lot of great teachings. Try to discern which of the two you plugged into.

# Being upbeat in a downbeat world

As a Spiritual Warrior (or any kind of warrior), your morale will determine your ability to act and fight the battle. If your morale is down, then there will be days you just don't want to get out of bed. You will want to lay down and play dead.

> *Guard your heart above all else for it determines the course of your life* (Prov 4:23)

The devil knows that if he can pull your morale down, he can disable you from being and doing all that Christ has for you. In the worst case of depression, he will lead you to self-destruction.

To stay upbeat doesn't start with the devil; it starts with us and the thoughts we entertain. *As you think, so you become.* What you think is also influenced by what you hear. Jesus says in Mark 4:24, "Be careful what you hear." The media and news channels, in particular, are full of bad news and real events, often sensationalised to keep viewers entertained. A little bad news can be good; it gives you issues you can pray about. Too much bad news, and you will think the world is ending tomorrow.

Too much negative input in your life depletes your morale, and if you entertain negative thoughts for long enough, it can lead to depression. It's like a diet of fatty foods being bad for your health. Your body needs nutrition, and your mind also requires a healthy diet of positive thoughts. One way to achieve great peace in your life is to generate positive thoughts and feelings.

Life and death are in the power of the tongue. If a declaration prayer can give birth to power and authority in Christ, can't negative declarations give birth to destruction? (*Whatever you confess with your mouth and believe in your heart*)

The last adversary to attack your morale is the self. What you think about yourself and the situation at hand? Out of all the misinformation coming out of the internet, we entertain more misinformation in our heads. The journey from downbeat to upbeat starts with challenging these negative thoughts. How bad is this situation, really? Will I die? If I die, I have the promise of salvation. Everlasting life with Jesus. No wonder the bible says, "In all things, we are more than conquerors".

## Oppression

The downbeat might not be coming from the media but from spouses, parents, or peers. Some criticism can be useful, but too much criticism only depletes your morale. When someone is critical of you, emotionally step back and ask yourself, "Is this criticism appropriate for the situation, or is this just their opportunity to vent?" There may be some basis for their criticism, but their opinion can be over the top. That's the thing. It is their opinion, and that does not necessarily represent the truth. The key to surviving this type of oppression is not to believe their lie. They may even be influenced by demonic spirits to attack you. This is a common strategy of the enemy to use someone close to you to attack you, which makes the whole event that much more painful.

## Pity Parties

Beware of pity parties. When things are not going well, it is very easy to focus on the negatives and either catastrophise them or twist the situation into something it's not. Your worldview at this point is distorted (See chapter five, Distortions of the Mind), and focusing on the negatives while ignoring the positives increases the likelihood of depression and disables you from solving the issue. In a pity party, you don't want someone to fix the problem; you just want pity.

## The Downward Spiral

There are two ways to enter a downward spin: suddenly through trauma and divorce, or slowly through gradual decay. Gradual decay occurs over time. You become tired and run down; there are endless demands on you. You feel confused and overwhelmed. Stress and anxiety lead to despair, which in turn leads to hopelessness and depression. Your life is on a downward spiral.

As more organisations try to do more with fewer people, mental breakdowns will become commonplace.

## The Upward Spiral

Tough times never last, but tough people do (Robert Schuller). Whatever the issues facing you today, they will be gone tomorrow.

There are six steps to spiralling upwards:

1. Establish boundaries
2. Correct your negative thinking
3. Correct diet
4. Correct exercise
5. Take sufficient rest
6. Spiritual revival

These lifestyle changes need to be reinforced with boundaries to stop the downward spiral. Then, as King David did, strengthen yourself in the Lord.

## *Boundaries*

Boundaries are a concept introduced in the book Boundaries by Henry Cloud. I strongly recommend this book. It's about setting limits: thus far and no more. Without work-life boundaries and limits, you could find yourself working twenty hours a day, six or seven days a week. Such a work-life is not sustainable. There may be times when you need to work long hours for a short period of time. However, this should not be for prolonged periods. If you are not getting enough sleep at night due to the demands of work, then you will need to enforce boundaries before you have a mental breakdown and lose both your job and your marriage.

Without limits or boundaries on ministry, the demands of the church and ministry can consume you. Between work life and ministry, is there any time left for family? Sadly, many young ministers of the gospel place ministry ahead of their family's needs, and eventually, the family disintegrates. [32]

*To everything, there is a season, a time for every purpose under heaven.* (Eccl 3:1)

Boundaries ensure that each aspect of your life has the right amount of time. A successful life is a balanced life.

## *Correct Thinking*

As you monitor your thought processes and purposely choose positive, healthy thoughts, don't be surprised if your mood lags behind your thinking. When a plane goes into a downward spiral, the pilot needs to apply the left aileron and right rudder to pull the plane out of the spin. However, the plane does not respond immediately; only after a period of wind flowing over its wings does the plane actually respond. So it is when you choose healthy thoughts over negative ones. It takes a little while for your emotions to catch up.

## *Diet*

Food is fuel for your body. Poor fuel clogs your inner workings, leaving you feeling lethargic, overweight, and miserable. Excess caffeine causes sleep degradation. Alcohol can temporarily lift your mood in small doses, but even then, alcohol in your bloodstream degrades the quality of your sleep. Where possible, eat at the same time each day and go to sleep and wake up at the same time each day. In this way, you will train your body to eat and sleep in a routine that maximises rest.

## *Exercise*

Adding exercise, particularly at the end of the day, not only lifts your mood but also helps ensure a good night's sleep. Your body is the temple of the Holy Spirit. You have an obligation to look after it. That does not mean going to the gym and lifting more weight than you can handle just to stroke your own ego. Wisdom lies in lifting small weights with high reps. This kind of training builds lasting endurance strength.

Where possible, do at least one workout a week that involves cardio. A good cardio workout helps with air flowing in and out of the lungs and keeps the heart strong.

## *Rest*

It is important to establish a routine where you go to bed at approximately the same time each night. The quality of your sleep is also important. Avoid drinking alcohol or eating just before bed. Evening exercise benefits some people, but others may become overtired and struggle to fall asleep. It comes down to whether you are a morning person or an evening person.

Rest isn't just about sleep; it also involves taking time out for yourself to engage in something you enjoy. God gave you this life to enjoy, not to endure. Find one thing you can do once a week that is solely for you to enjoy yourself.

## *Spiritual Revival*

Feeling low and at the point of despair is often an indication that you need spiritual revival. King David found himself in a desperate low in 1 Samual 30:1-6.

> *David and his men reached Ziklag on the third day. Now the Amalekites had raided the Negev and Ziklag. They had attacked Ziklag and burned it, and had taken captive the women and everyone else in it, both young and old. They killed none of them, but carried them off as they went on their way.*
>
> *When David and his men reached Ziklag, they found it destroyed by fire and their wives and sons and daughters taken captive. So David and his men wept aloud until they had no strength left to weep. David's two wives had been captured—Ahinoam of Jezreel and Abigail, the widow of Nabal of Carmel. David was greatly distressed because the men were talking of stoning him; each one was bitter in spirit because of his sons and daughters. But David found strength in the Lord his God.*

Here, we have David's own men threatening to stone him. Everyone is exhausted from marching for three days. He has lost his wife and children. Needless to say, David has reached a point where his morale is at an all-time low. But David found strength in the Lord his God.

It is important to note that David's men weren't encouraging. His pastor was nowhere to be seen, and his wives certainly weren't there to cheer him on. David needed encouragement, just like we need it when adversity strikes. Self-encouragement starts with stopping all negative thoughts, even if they are true. David's men were planning to stone him, but that's not where he focused his attention. Instead, he strengthened himself in the Lord and sought God for spiritual guidance and strength.

Every day, I strengthen myself in the Lord and prepare for the battle. How can you find strength in the Lord your God?

Start by meditating on the following scripts. Can you identify times when God has been gracious to you? Will he not be gracious again?

> *And my God will supply every need of yours according to his riches in glory in Christ Jesus.* (Philippians 4:19)

And my God will supply some of my needs. No, every need. According to His riches. If He's God almighty, how rich are we talking about?

> *Fear not, for I am with you; be not dismayed, for I am your God; I will strengthen you, I will help you, I will uphold you with my righteous right hand.* (Isaiah 41:10)

I am with you. Who is with you? God? God almighty? For he is your God. If the God who is almighty, all-powerful, the creator of Heaven and Earth, is your God, then whom should you fear?

> *"My grace is all you need, for my power is the greatest when you are weak."* (2 Corinthians 12:9)

Are you feeling weak? Then His power is great and His grace is deep, what more do you need?

> *"My flesh and my heart may fail, but God is the strength of my heart and my portion forever."* (Psalm 73:26)

Are you feeling run down and physically weak? Is your heart failing you? God is your strength, ever-present help in times of trouble.

> *"Do not grieve, for the joy of the Lord is your strength."* (Nehemiah 8:10)

When you're alone and worshipping Him in that quiet place, you bring Him joy. At the same time, you receive joy—the joy of the Lord, which is your strength.

> *Be strong and courageous. Do not fear or be in dread of them, for it is the Lord your God who goes with you. He will not leave you or forsake you* (Deuteronomy 31:6)

This word of encouragement came to the Jews just prior to their going into battle against a fierce enemy, many of whom were giants. Are you facing giants? Issues too great for you? Just as this encouragement was meant for the Jews prior to battle, so it is for you. The Lord your God goes with you. He will not leave you or forsake you. He loves you.

Consider Philippians 4:8. Following Paul's instructions on thought life prevents you from dwelling on the negative and helps maintain healthy morale.

> *Finally, brothers and sisters, whatever is true, whatever is noble, whatever is right, whatever is pure, whatever is lovely, whatever is admirable—if anything is excellent or praiseworthy—think about such things.* (Phil 4:8)

Meditating on how God has blessed you will take your mind off the negatives of this world. Are you still breathing? It's His breath in your lungs. You can thank Him that you're alive. Do you have food to eat and water to drink? You're in better shape than many of those in Africa who are trying to escape a war zone. Have you accepted Jesus Christ as your Lord and Saviour? If so, then you've inherited eternal life. You are in better shape than ninety percent of the Earth's population.

Whatever issues you face today are temporal. They will be gone tomorrow.

# PART VI

# The Way of the Devil

The devil does not come except to steal and to kill and to destroy. (John 10:10)

# Know your enemy

By now you know yourself. You know something of the world. It's time to get to know the enemy. If you know your enemy and know yourself, you will never be defeated in battle. (Sun Tzu, The Art of War)

> "How you are fallen from heaven, O Lucifer, son of the morning! How you are cut down to the ground, You who weakened the nations! For you have said in your heart: 'I will ascend into heaven, I will exalt my throne above the stars of God; I will also sit on the mount of the congregation On the farthest sides of the north; I will ascend above the heights of the clouds, I will be like the Most High.' Yet you shall be brought down to Sheol, To the lowest depths of the Pit. (Isaiah 14:12-15)

Lucifer (Satan) is described as the Son of the Morning. He led worship in heaven. Let's look at how else the bible describes Lucifer.

> *You were the seal of perfection, Full of wisdom and perfect in beauty. You were in Eden, the garden of God.* (Ezek 28:11)

Note the first two words: "You were". That's past tense. Satan was a great and highly esteemed angel in heaven until pride and vanity filled his heart, causing him to become self-deluded. He thinks he will be like the Most High, taking all the honour and glory for himself. To achieve this goal, he led a rebellion in heaven, convincing a third of the angels to follow him. Derek Prince thinks, and I agree with his conjecture, that the third of the angels he persuaded were those who reported to him.[33] So today, we have a kingdom set up by Satan in direct opposition to God, with a similar structure to what he commanded when he led worship.

## THE FIRST TEMPTATION

Satan and his fallen angels then came to Earth to attack mankind. Why? Because he knows how much God loves mankind, created in His image, and he knows that destroying mankind will hurt God more than anything else he could do. He and his fallen angels hate us with perfect hatred. His first attack is in the Garden of Eden with the first temptation.

> *Now the serpent was more crafty than any of the wild animals the Lord God had made. He said to the woman, Did God really say, 'You must not eat from any tree in the garden?'"* (Gen 3:1)

Notice that there is no mention of Adam in this verse. It would seem that in this instance, Eve is alone in the garden and is unable to concur with Adam when Satan sows his seeds of doubt. Satan starts with, "Did God really say?". He's questioning both Eve's ability to hear from God and God's integrity to be honest.

> *The woman said to the serpent, "We may eat fruit from the trees in the garden, ³ but God did say, 'You must not eat fruit from the tree that is in the middle of the garden, and you must not touch it, or you will die.'"* (Gen 3:2)

> *You will not certainly die, the serpent said to the woman. For God knows that when you eat from it your eyes will be opened and you will be like God, knowing good and evil.* (Gen 3:4-5)

When Eve enters into a dialogue with Satan, she is taking the bait. By responding to Satan and reaffirming what God said, this provides grounds for Satan to distort the trust. Satan knows when she is ready to receive in her mind a direct denial of God's word and a total misrepresentation of God's purpose: "You will not surely die."

It's a two-step process, starting with half-truths, which lay the foundation for accepting a complete lie.

By sowing these seeds of doubt, Satan is saying, "Can you trust God?" Satan's attack upon God's motives (Gen 3:5) in withholding the forbidden tree is an attack upon his character. Satan is declaring, "God is not honest. He is taking advantage of your ignorance."

Eve begins to act independently of God. Men and women want to live the way they choose to live, not as God declares they should live. In essence, they want to be their own gods. Eve could have stopped the dialogue at this point and saved the day.

After sowing doubt and half-truths, the stage is set for an outright lie. The self-centred benefit of the fruit blinds Eve. She now chooses to ignore God's command, oblivious to the consequences. Had she known the consequences, she would never have taken the fruit. So it is with us; if we knew the consequences of that sin, we would never have done it. Self-deception and selfishness lie behind every successful temptation.

Did you know that the average temptation lasts only seven seconds? This means that if you can resist the devil for seven seconds and then begin thinking of something else, the entire temptation will dissolve and the snare of the enemy will be destroyed.

## DEMONIC HIERARCHY

The Bible doesn't have much to say about Satan's demonic hierarchy, but it does imply a well-organized structure. It is highly likely that when Satan rebelled, he persuaded a third of the angels who reported to him to follow him. What the Bible does not clarify is whether other heavenly hosts besides angels rebelled with Satan. The Bible refers to two entities: fallen angels and unclean spirits, also known as demons. Let me explain further.

The Bible clearly indicates in the book of Genesis that the Sons of God went into the daughters of men. They needed a body to do this. In the New Testament, Matt 12:43 speaks of unclean spirits going out of a man and traveling through dry places seeking rest, then returning to the host from which they were cast out. So, unclean spirits don't have a body but need one. These are two different entities. The demons are, therefore, the foot soldiers, while the fallen angels become the officers of Satan's army.

The same hierarchy that applied in heaven also applies today in the fallen world. Fallen angels are given authority over nations, cities, and regions within those nations. Within a city, demons have authority over cultural groups. Satan's kingdom is well-structured.

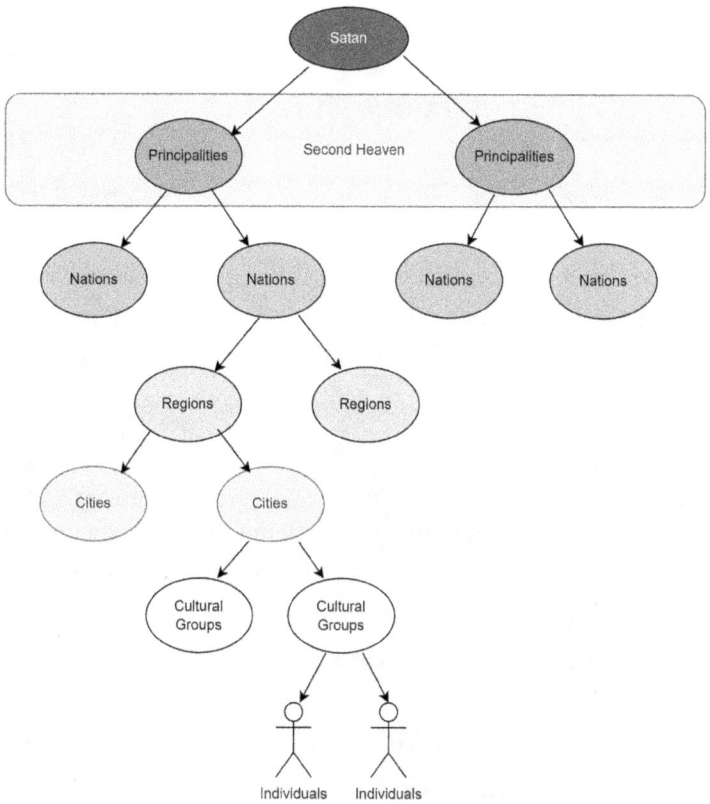

Figure 15.1 – The Demonic Hierarchy

Paul in Ephesians 6:12 speaks of our struggle against spiritual forces of evil in heavenly places. In Daniel 10:20, the angel Gabriel is returning to fight the prince of Persia. If the prince of Persia were an earthly prince or a spirit on the earth, he would not need to return. From this, we can gather that there are spiritual forces of Satan actively fighting in the spiritual realms, also referred to as the second heaven. The rest of Satan's cohorts are deployed on the earth, and these are the demons we face in our daily battles. You have dominion over them and don't have to put up with their antics.

## Demonic Nature

The devil comes to kill, rob, and destroy. His primary weapon is deception. He doesn't have a lot of other weapons. Once his plots are discovered, he tends to flee. The Bible says he is the father of lies. While he can't read your thoughts, he can read your moods and emotions. If you entertain thoughts of fear or anger, then they will eventually engage your heart, and that becomes a foothold for the devil.

He can plant thoughts in your mind to influence your thinking. He can tempt you to sin, but he can't make you do it. He can spiritually oppress you, affecting your thoughts and emotions and influencing your will in a single attack. This can manifest as sudden depression without a cause.

His demons take time to study your strengths and weaknesses. They learn the best ways to bring you down by attacking your most vulnerable areas. They then look for a time when you are most exposed. An example is a married man with a lust problem who is asked to work late. Satan orchestrates the event so the sexy office girl has to work with him, leaving the two alone. If she comes on to him, there will be a real spiritual battle for that man to leave the office with his integrity.

The devil does not play fair, and he does not take prisoners. He will wait until you are tired, exhausted, and run down, and then look for an opportunity to kick you in the guts.

They cause discord, division, and torment, inflict illness of various kinds, and can drive you to mental insanity. Suicide is only one step away.

Demons are not omnipresent; they can only be in one place at a time. Satan's best strategy is to get you thinking in self-defeating, negative terms. Once he starts your downward spiral, he can step back and move on to someone else.

Some of Satan's demons aren't that smart. They certainly aren't wise, or they wouldn't have chosen the losing team.

Satan's demons are already defeated, thanks to the work of the cross. They have no future. Christ was not crucified for them. There is no plan of redemption for them. Their eternity consists of torture in the lake of fire, forever. These creatures are truly doomed and wish nothing more than for you to suffer the same fate.

But God, filled with mercy and grace because of His deep, wonderful, and intense love for you, has provided redemption in Jesus Christ. You have a future that's bright and wonderful, beyond anything you could hope or imagine. Is it any wonder the demons are a little jealous?

## God's Protection

God sets limits on the seas. Thus far and no more. Similarly, when Satan was allowed to oppress Job, he was allowed to afflict his body but not take his life. God sets limits on Satan, thus far and no more.

*God is faithful; He will not let you be tempted beyond what you can bear.* (1 Cor 10:13)

It is well known in warfare that to know your enemy and to know yourself, you will never lose in battle. The devil studies us, knows our weaknesses, and has accumulated much intel on us. What do we know about Satan's demons? The Bible says the enemy comes to steal, rob, and destroy. Not a whole lot was said beyond that. Why? Demons are agents of evil on

Earth. They serve two purposes. They impact the unsaved to bring them to the fullness of iniquity. They afflict the saved to test their faith, to cause them to fight back and become stronger. God does not want all of Satan's demons cast into the pit, yet. The reason the Bible isn't more explicit on the nature of demons is that God needs to protect them from US.

## AUTHORITY

Demons are not all-powerful, are not omnipresent, and have no future. We, as Christians, are loved by God and predestined before the beginning of time to be adopted as children of God. As adopted children, we have inherited power and authority.

> *And [I pray] that the eyes of your heart [the very center and core of your being] may be enlightened [flooded with light by the Holy Spirit], so that you will know and cherish the hope [the divine guarantee, the confident expectation] to which He has called you, the riches of His glorious inheritance in the saints (God's people), and [so that you will begin to know] what the immeasurable and unlimited and surpassing greatness of His [active, spiritual] power is in us who believe.* (Eph 1:18-19 AMP)

We have power and authority over demons to cast them out and trample them underfoot. However, most of us may not possess the authority to overcome territorial spirits, which are, in fact, fallen angels and those residing in the second heaven. If we did, the church of God could confine every demon in Satan's army to the bottomless pit in just a few weeks. Then, how would the end times come to pass?

All Christians have authority over unclean spirits (Satan's foot soldiers) by taking authority over them. In this way, when we put on the full armour of God, we can withstand the attacks of the enemy. To take authority over territorial spirits requires a greater level of authority that comes from the anointing. In this situation, God anoints you for a purpose, you receive a greater level of spiritual authority, and then God provides instructions on how and when you are to use that authority.

See chapter twenty-three, Intercession that Backfires, for details on the implications of stepping out without sufficient authority to win the battle.

## FINAL COMMENTS

The Bible is very clear about what we need to understand: live a righteous life and spread the Gospel to all nations. Love God and love your neighbour as yourself. However, when it comes to demons and demonology, the Bible doesn't provide much information on the subject.

You don't need to know the name of the demon to cast it out of someone. When the Bible talks about a spirit of fear or a spirit of lust, that refers to a type of spirit, not the demon's name. You don't need to know the demonic hierarchy in depth. All you really need to know is that you have authority over the day-to-day demons that are attacking you. You do not have authority over the principalities occupying the second heaven, and attacking them may have dire consequences.

God uses Satan's fallen angels as agents of evil on the earth. See here how He uses a spirit to be a lying tongue in the mouth of Ahab's prophets.

> *The Lord asked, "Who will go and deceive King Ahab so that he attacks Ramoth Gilead and he dies there?" Many of the angels suggested different things. Then a spirit came and stood*

in front of the Lord. The spirit said, "I will deceive Ahab." The Lord asked him, "How will you do it?" The spirit said, "I will give a message to all Ahab's prophets. I will cause them to speak lies." The Lord said, "Go and deceive King Ahab, as you have said. He will do what you say." (1 King 22:20)

God has a purpose even for Satan's fallen angels on the earth. I believe this is why Paul in Eph 6:13 says: *after you have done everything, to* **stand**. He is not telling us to aggressively attack Satan's kingdom until every demon is locked up in the bottomless pit. If we did, then who would God use on the earth as agents of evil? How would the End Times come to pass? Our enemy is fulfilling a purpose on the earth that we don't fully understand yet. But one thing the Bible is clear on is that we must stand and hold our ground.

## WARNING

In my pursuit of knowledge about the enemy, I found three groups of books. The first group consists of books on demonology written by Christians that offer valuable insights. Many of these authors are ex-Satanists. (Unmasking the Devil by John Ramirez is a good source.) The second group includes writings by individuals claiming to be Christians and to possess unique insights into the spiritual realm, but their books are filled with rubbish. The third group comprises active Satanists, whose perspective is to use witchcraft against other malevolent groups. It reflects the old paradigm of the white witch versus the black witch. Beware, there is no distinction between white witchcraft and black witchcraft; it's simply witchcraft, and it's evil. Reading these types of books can result in demonic oppression and create an opening for the devil. This is why many who embark on a quest to understand demons ultimately end up losing their very faith in God.

# Schemes of the Devil

It's time to get to know some of the schemes of our enemy. *"In order that Satan might not outwit us. For we are not unaware of his schemes"* (2 Cor 2:11)

This chapter does not cover every scheme of the enemy but provides varied examples of some of his strategies, along with food for thought on how he may be oppressing you. They are certainly relevant if you are engaged in the battle and have the devil's attention.

The devil's schemes can be divided into two categories: inner conflict and outer conflict. In your personal life, this corresponds to internal thoughts and feelings for inner conflict, and to the external environment for outer conflict.

The same principle applies to the family. The inner conflict is the conflict that the devil uses to stir up strife. The end goal is to divide and conquer. The outer conflict is an external stimulus that causes strife and stress. It could be an unexpected bill or fine that attacks your finances, a sickness or injury to a loved one, or a conflict with a neighbour. Satan orchestrates external events to add to the internal stress and strife. His end goal is your demise.

The same principle applies at the church level. Satan plants wolves in sheep's clothing that don't spare the flock. Self-seeking people end up in positions of authority and will try to manipulate the direction of the church, out of the will of God. On the external conflict level, disgruntled ex-members and media will, at times, attack the leadership of the church. Satan's goal is to disable the church from being effective in the community.

## *Prayer for the Church to smash Satan's plans*

*Father, I pray for my pastor, that you will give him strength and courage; clarity of mind to know your will, and that your will be done expediently in the church. I command under the authority of Jesus Christ for all demonic oppression to be expelled from my pastor, his family, and the church, and all seeds of the devil will be exposed and removed, in Jesus's name.*

### INCREMENTAL CHANGE – INCREMENTAL SIN

You can put a frog suddenly in a pot of boiling water, and it will jump out immediately. But if you start with the water being tepid and slowly increase the temperature, the frog becomes oblivious to the change and slowly cooks to death. Satan uses this approach on two levels: personally and socially.

Imagine you start clubbing on a Friday night. As you go to bars, you have a few drinks, but no more than three throughout the night. You dance with a few girls, and it's just a bit of fun. So far, nothing untoward has occurred in this story. After several months, someone offers you a puff on their joint in the toilets. Just one smoke — what harm could it do? The smoke in the toilet then becomes a weekly habit. Several months pass, and one Friday, the joint is replaced with a line of Coke. Maybe it's a little exaggerated, but I think you get the gist.

If the dialogue above sounds unlikely, I have a friend whose sister tried heroin just once, thinking that once would be okay, and she became instantly addicted, spending the next twenty years on the streets working as a prostitute to pay for her heroin addiction.

The incremental change in society can often be less obvious. We know from the book of Revelation that there will come a time when you can only buy and sell goods if you have a mark of the beast with which to trade. The only way to reach a point where you need a mark instead of money is if the global monetary system collapses. Satan wants to orchestrate this, and it can only be accomplished through incremental change so as not to upset the Christians who read their Bible. That journey started with an increase in credit instead of savings: buying now and paying later. This has become a widely accepted practice. As the use of credit and credit cards increased, society began transitioning to a cashless environment, which was further reinforced when COVID-19 hit. Now, there's an additional shift toward cryptocurrencies, which are not tied to gold, silver, or the dollar. The only conclusion I can reach is that Satan's plan is intact and progressing well. (God, please help us)

The key takeaway is to stay alert for incremental changes in your own life that may lead you down the path of unethical practices. The earlier you break the progression, the easier it will be to stay free.

## The Young Lion

Psalm 91:13 says: "You will trample on Lions and the cobra". For many years, I have ignored this scripture as I don't have any lions living near me. Or do I?

John Ramirez, in his book Unmasking the Devil, expounds on this scripture better than anyone else.

> The Young Lion – a smooth trap, hidden so you don't see the impending danger. It's a small sin you think you have under control, and **you do not**. When you play around with or entertain a "young lion," what you do not end up killing and putting away from you now will end up killing you. When it's full-grown, it becomes the lion or dragon that Psalm 91:13 describes. That's how the enemy finds a way to build strongholds in your life.

Be on guard for the young lions. One day, they will grow up.

## Proxy by Friend or Spouse

Have you ever woken up in the morning only to have your spouse or someone close to you bite your head off? Perhaps they have some justification for their outburst. Do not engage emotionally. The moment you engage your emotions, you react, and the situation escalates. Detach yourself from the emotions of the moment and ask yourself: "Are their emotions out of context with reality?" "Could this be a demonic spirit influencing their thoughts and emotions, or could it be an emotional projection? An emotional projection occurs when an event triggers suppressed emotions from prior trauma, and what you are facing is an emotional dump.

Whatever the source, it is important to respond rather than react to the situation. Allow them to vent. Once they've expressed all their negative emotions, you can counsel them with logic and reasoning. Ask questions like: "Has this ever happened before?" "Why do you feel so strongly about this issue?". If the questions cause the issue to escalate again, then refrain from asking further questions; instead, wait for peace to return before attempting to find the root cause. If it is a spiritual influence, it is often short-lived.

## Attacking Your Relationships

The demons study our behaviour to understand how and when we are most vulnerable. They prey on relationships where both partners feel the need to win the argument and believe they must have the last word. In this scenario, it is easy for conflicts to continue and escalate into violence.

Winning an argument doesn't win a friend. Having the last word doesn't win an argument.

Little secrets are another foothold for the devil to exploit in a relationship. If you are hiding any dark secrets from your past, it is best that you bring them into the light. If you don't, the devil will. When the devil brings it to the light, you won't receive the mercy you do by confessing it yourself.

## Divide and Conquer

I was going through a rough patch in my marriage when the Lord spoke to me about this strategy. He said, "The devil's number one strategy is to divide and conquer. If he divides, will he not also conquer?"

I stopped and started to consider all the marriages in my church that had ended in divorce. Many of those spouses are not going to a church of any kind.

> *Every kingdom divided against itself is brought to desolation; and every city or house divided against itself shall not stand* (Matt 12:25)

This scripture is not only relevant for marriages but also specifically for the church as a whole. The greatest problem facing the church today is division.

> *With all lowliness and gentleness, with longsuffering, bearing with one another in love* (Eph 4:2)

No church is perfect. You won't always agree with the pastor. Sometimes, the pastor will know better than you because he has heard from God or sees the bigger picture. At other times, the pastor might be wrong because, after all, he is human, just like you. Unless the pastor is violating God's law, you have an obligation to follow his instruction as Jesus's anointed representative.

## Doubts about Salvation

The god of this world blinds the minds of believers and sows seeds of doubt: "Are you really saved?" "How could God possibly love you after what you've done?"

It is important to understand that salvation is not merely a feeling. Just because we feel guilty (shameful) for something we've done does not mean God has cast us off.

> *You are my servant; I have chosen you and have not cast you away.* (Isa 41:9)

We must understand once and for all that:

1. A Christian is still a Christian even if he is struggling with a serious sin problem in his life (1 Cor. 5:1–5; 11:30–32; 1 John 2:1–2)

2. A Christian is still a Christian even if he is struggling with a serious "world" problem in his life (2 Tim. 4:10)
3. A Christian is still a Christian even if he is struggling with serious demonic problems in his life *(Acts 5:1-10; Tim 5:9-15)*[34]

> *If we confess our sins, he is faithful and just and will forgive us our sins and purify us from all unrighteousness.*
> (1 John 1:9)

God is eager for us to confess our sins and come back to that close relationship we once had.

## ATTACKING YOUR SELF-ESTEEM

Throughout much of our lives, we've had a variety of people speak into our lives. Sometimes this occurs to our benefit and other times it does not. When people speak positive words, they build us up. Conversely, when people speak negative words, they tear us down, but only if we choose to believe them. Sometimes, the individuals sharing their words are significant figures, such as our parents.

When I was still in my teens, I came home from school and told my dad I wanted to be a computer engineer when I left school. He told me I wasn't smart enough. I had to leave school and get a job. He told me, "Get a trade of some kind." "Who needs a computer anyway?" I didn't believe him, but I pursued my dream. Had I believed him, my life would have turned out very differently.

So, even parents get it wrong. How much less should we listen to our peers and colleagues who are overly critical? Constructive criticism is useful; it corrects us so that the next time we do it better. However, being overly critical tears us down. Over time, we become our own critics, and harsh critics at that. We start thinking, "I'm stupid," "I'm ugly," "I'll never be any good." This is where Satan now gets a foothold. Notice that when you make just one screwup, that one thing keeps playing over and over in your mind. Satan reinforces your feelings of guilt and shame to the point where you believe you are stupid and a failure.

If he can get you thinking in these terms, he has created a downward spiral into depression. He can then take his hands off as you are set for self-destruction and, at the very least, won't be effective for Christ.

If you see this pattern of thinking, take authority. Pray, "Satan, by the authority of Jesus Christ, as a child of God, I command you to leave me now. I close the door to my mind that you have had access through. I ask the Holy Spirit to come and fill me afresh."

Now, forgive yourself. It is okay to make mistakes; that's how you learn in life. It's not okay to make the same mistake repeatedly. If you find yourself caught in recurring sin, read chapter nineteen on strongholds. If your sin has reached the stage of bondage, you may need some help from a counsellor or pastor.

Lastly, stop entertaining negative thoughts.

> *Finally, brethren, whatever things are true, whatever things are noble, whatever things are just, whatever things are pure, whatever things are lovely, whatever things are of good report, if there is any virtue and if there is anything praiseworthy—meditate on these things* (Phil 4:8)

If you allow Satan to, he will lower your morale until you find yourself in despair, and the situation feels hopeless. Stop him before he gets a foothold.

## Fatigue

We are harassed, resisted, afflicted, tormented, tripped up, sabotaged, and often defeated. Over time, we become weary and discouraged. We begin to suffer battle fatigue and become critical, bitter, cynical, and defeated. While you have self-control, you are in a position of power and can make rational decisions. Once your emotions engage and you lose self-control, you find yourself in a position of weakness.

> *Now David was greatly distressed, for the people spoke of stoning him, because the soul of all the people was grieved, every man for his sons and his daughters. But David strengthened himself in the LORD his God* (1 Sam 30:6)

We see in this scripture that David and his men were exhausted after marching three days to return to Ziglag, only to find that the city had been burned and the occupants taken captive. David's own men wanted to stone him. The key to recovery lay in strengthening himself in the Lord, worshipping Him for what He has done and, in faith, for what He will do. From this, David was able to gain the strength and courage to pursue the enemy and recover all that was lost.

The devil will also get you fighting the wrong battle or the wrong issue, so there is no fight left in you when the real issue raises its head. At other times, he will create both the problem and the solution. However, the solution is worse than the original problem. In this way, he ensnares you. An example is introducing you to meditation to help cope with stress. You overcome the stress, but open yourself up to demonic influence through Eastern meditation.

## DISTORTING THE WORD OF GOD

This can take two forms: quoting verses from the Bible out of context and blending the Word of God with occult or new age doctrine. The chapter on Misinformation provided examples of the former. The latter form often appeals to those who have grown tired of traditional church teachings. Such entwined teachings typically give rise to cults, where the leader is both very evangelical and controlling. The Mormon church is an example of this.

## DREAMS & VISIONS – FROM THE ENEMY

For a long time, I was going to a large church in Sydney and was regularly giving 10% of my income as a tithe. But I fell for a scam and lost a substantial amount of money. I was left with a tough decision: eat or pay my tithe? I had been strongly encouraged to give 10% of my salary, and I felt compelled to follow Malachi 3:10: Bring your tithes into the storehouse, so there will be food in My House.

So, for the next four years, we ate and paid our tithe with a line of credit, thereby continually increasing our debt. The stage was set, but not for a move of God, but a move of the devil.

One night in bed, I had a dream of a petrol station advertising not the price of petrol but the price of oil per barrel. There were two values: $57.70 and $75.00. I knew these figures were in US dollars since oil trades in USD. At the time of the vision, the price was $60.50 per barrel, and the last previous high was $71.00, which represented a $4 increase on the previous high. Oil was progressing upwards. I did my due diligence, and fundamentally, oil companies were having to drill offshore in deeper water as current supplies were drying up.

It all seemed like a safe play, and since we were faithfully tithing, this was God's way of blessing us. So, I opened a CFD account that exposed us to futures contracts on oil. I set a conditional buy price at $57.70. Should the price of oil fall to $57.70, then we would be in the market. If it never reached $57.70, then it wasn't from God. Within a week, the price of oil fell, and we were in the market with six thousand barrels. Oil traded on a three percent margin, so it cost us just $10386 to hold that position. With leveraged accounts like CFDs and futures, you open a position with a small amount of money, and then your broker deposits money into your account when the price rises and withdraws money when it falls. In our case, the price rose, and money was deposited into our account. Then, for each $2 rise in the oil price, we bought another two thousand barrels. By the time oil hit $61.70, we were holding ten thousand barrels. I had calculated that by the time oil hit $75, we would be debt-free. This was definitely God. Nothing could stop us now, nothing.

Then, the price started to head south. Money was being debited from our account. I exited the trade at $55.00 a barrel and suffered a significant loss. Woe was I.

This was a perfectly executed plan by the devil. At no time did I seek confirmation from God or His word. I did not discuss this with my pastor or anyone else. I was completely self-deluded.

There are a few lessons that can be learned from these misfortunes. Using a line of credit or borrowing money to pay a tithe is stupid. We should all give what we can afford, not what we can't afford. The legalism of tithing was an Old Testament doctrine. If you are going to live by the law of Judaism, then you need to adopt all the Old Testament laws, not just tithing. The truth is we are saved by faith in Jesus Christ and by grace, not by law.

> *God loves a cheerful giver.* (2 Cor 9:6)

After the oil incident, I went on a quest. How can I hear from God? After reading about six different books, I came to just one conclusion: Matt 7:16 *You will know them by their fruits.* AND Matt 7:18: *A good tree cannot bear bad fruit, nor can a bad tree bear good fruit.*

In my case, it was difficult to see the fruit as bad unless I started to question, "Did I really hear from God?". At this point, I could have asked God for some confirmation. I could have gone to my pastor for advice. Pride and arrogance blinded me to those choices and the possibility that this was not from God.

The devil will use dreams to talk to you, just like God can. Three things you can do to help discern who the message is from.

1. Ask yourself, "If this were to come to pass, what would it achieve?" Does it produce good or bad fruit?
2. Ask God for confirmation either in his word or by the mouth of someone who does not know the situation.
3. Talk it through with your pastor.

Lastly, the closer you walk with God, the easier you will be able to discern who is speaking.

## Attacking Your Finances

Time and money are the two resources you have to sow into the kingdom of God. The devil knows this and will attack your finances if you are sowing into the kingdom. If you are not sowing into the kingdom of God, then I think you have bigger problems.

Types of financial attacks include:

- Encouraging poor financial decisions
- Promoting greed and materialism
- Stealing through circumstances
- Fear and anxiety about money
- Blocking financial breakthroughs

Overcome financial attacks by:

- Pray for Wisdom (James 1:5) – Ask God for financial guidance and discernment.
- Be a Good Steward (Proverbs 21:5) – Budget wisely, avoid debt, and manage money with discipline.
- Give Generously (2 Cor 9:6) – Many believe that giving opens doors for financial blessings.
- Break Generational Curses – If financial struggles run in the family, pray against generational cycles of poverty.
- Declare God's Promises – Speak and believe scriptures about provision (Philippians 4:19, Deuteronomy 8:18).
- Resist the Enemy (James 4:7) – Stand firm in faith and refuse to let fear or deception control financial decisions.

## Attacking Your Workplace

Attacking your workplace is another means of attacking your finances. The devil's plan is to introduce strife and increase your stress, which overflows into your family life. If the devil can get you working hard enough, with enough stress, and for long enough, he knows you will have a breakdown, which will likely lead to loss of job and income.

The flow-on effect of this is financial stress to the family. He's not done with you yet. Just as a murderer will twist the knife after plunging it into your abdomen, so the devil will continue to attack your marriage as it is likely to be at its most vulnerable point.

Attacks in the workplace can also manifest as psychological or verbal abuse from colleagues. This behaviour often occurs when your coworkers know you are a Christian and perceive a threat. Consider this: why do your religious beliefs elicit a response from your colleagues? Either they feel threatened deep down, or the demon manipulating them feels threatened. Either way, hold your head high. As God's ambassador on Earth, you represent Christ in the workplace. Their taunts won't endure long. Eventually, a day will come when disaster strikes them, and they will seek you for comfort. On that day, you will be that light that shines.

# PART V

## Warfare

For we do not struggle against flesh and blood, but against the rules, against the authorities, against the powers of this dark world and against the spiritual forces of evil in the heavenly realms. (Eph 6:12)

# The Battle

We have covered the works of the flesh, the way of the world and the way of the devil, and seen these are three separate adversaries. They actually all work together for one common cause; to separate you from God.

Enticements to sin may begin as fleshly desires, which are then reinforced by the world. Meanwhile, demonic powers will try to influence our hearts and minds to further push us toward sin.

At a world level, the demonic powers that rule this world can and do influence people's thinking and emotions to create worldviews. If everyone else is doing it, we are likely to as well.

All three adversaries are working together but not necessarily all the time.

In Luke 4:13, we see that after a period of tempting Jesus, the devil left him until an opportune time. It's not in Satan's interest to continually attack you all the time. If he did, you would be constantly on your guard.

However, after a period of attack, he will leave you for an opportune time, when your defences are down and you aren't expecting an attack.

## Opposing Forces

I mentioned earlier in chapter fifteen how Satan and his demons serve as God's agents of evil on the Earth. He uses Satan to test the loyalty of His people through various trials. He uses Satan to influence the unbeliever and to keep him self-focused in order to fulfil his iniquity. God needs Satan to fulfil end times prophecies. His main strategy is deception.

### Satan's Attack

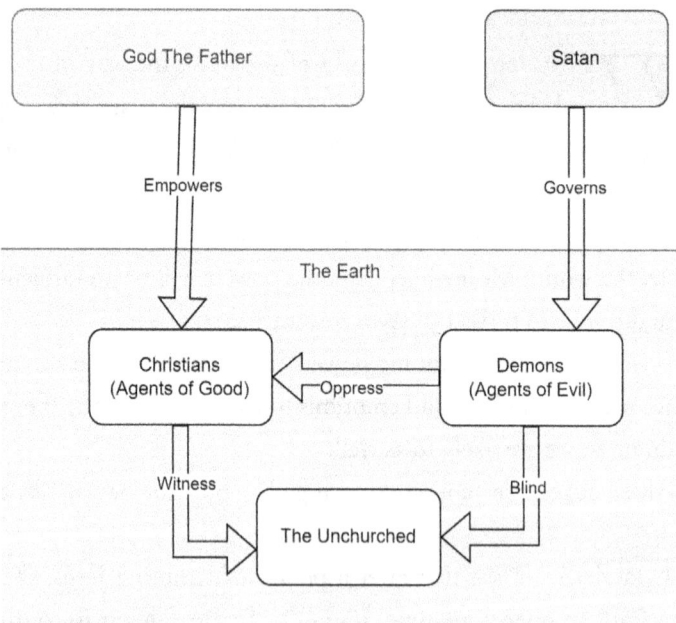

Figure 17.1 – The influence of forces on the Earth

The unbelievers are all blinded by Satan so that they cannot, in themselves, receive the gospel.

> *But even if our gospel is veiled, it is veiled to those who are perishing* (2 Cor 4:3-4)

They are all under the power of the evil one (1 John 5:19), in his grip and under his dominion. Asleep in the arms of Satan, they are all enslaved to a world system controlled by Satan (John 12:31; 14:30; 16:11; 1 John 5:19). They have surrendered to the prince of the power of the air, and their life is energised by the power of evil supernaturalism.

## LIMITS ARE SET

Just as the ocean has limits, God puts limits on Satan regarding what he can and cannot do. Equally, he puts limits on us.

Let's see how this plays out in the story of Job. Job is a man the bible refers to as blameless and upright, who fears God and shuns evil.

> *Now there was a day when the sons of God came to present themselves before the Lord, and Satan also came among them. And the Lord said to Satan, "From where do you come?" So Satan answered the Lord and said, "From going to and fro on the earth, and from walking back and forth on it." (Job 1:6)*
>
> *Then the Lord said to Satan, "Have you considered My servant Job, that there is none like him on the earth, a blameless and upright man, one who fears God and shuns evil?"* (Job 1:8)

Not only is there a dialogue between God and our adversary, Satan, but God is enticing Satan to attack Job. In fact, God showcases Job as one of his most faithful servants on the Earth.

> *So Satan answered the Lord and said, "Does Job fear God for nothing? Have You not made a hedge around him, around his household, and around all that he has on every side? You have blessed the work of his hands, and his possessions have increased in the land. But now, stretch out Your hand and touch all that he has, and he will surely curse You to Your face!"* (Job 1:9)

Satan calls out that God has placed a hedge around Job, his house, and all that he possesses. Satan has no foothold for an attack; he is completely protected on every side. He then tries to entice God to strike Job without cause.

> *And the Lord said to Satan, "Behold, all that he has is in your power; only do not lay a hand on his person." So Satan went out from the presence of the Lord.* (Job 1:12)

God gives Satan access rights to Job.

> *Now there was a day when his sons and daughters were eating and drinking wine in their oldest brother's house; and a messenger came to Job and said, "The oxen were plowing and the donkeys feeding beside them, when the Sabeans raided them and took them away—indeed they have killed the servants with the edge of the sword; and I alone have escaped to tell you!"* (Job 1:13)

> *While he was still speaking, another also came and said, "The fire of God fell from heaven and burned up the sheep and the servants, and consumed them; and I alone have escaped to tell you!"* (Job 1:16)

> *While he was still speaking, another also came and said, "The Chaldeans formed three bands, raided the camels and took them away, yes, and killed the servants with the edge of the sword; and I alone have escaped to tell you!"* (Job 1:17)

> *While he was still speaking, another also came and said, "Your sons and daughters were eating and drinking wine in their oldest brother's house, and suddenly a great wind came from across the wilderness and struck the four corners of the house, and it fell on the young people, and they are dead; and I alone have escaped to tell you!"* (Job 1:18)

Notice the simultaneous attacks on multiple fronts, aimed at leaving Job overwhelmed with grief. It is important to note that Job is not just grieving for the loss of his family alone; he is also grieving for his servants, having known many of them for many years. Additionally, this is apart from the loss of his great wealth.

> *Then Job arose, tore his robe, and shaved his head; and he fell to the ground and worshipped. And he said: "Naked I came from my mother's womb, And naked shall I return there. The Lord gave, and the Lord has taken away; Blessed be the name of the Lord."* (Job 1:20)

What an extraordinarily wise response. He does not blame God but blesses God. On the other hand, there was no mercy shown by Satan, no truce or negotiation. His attacks were pre-emptive and decisive. Any thought of compromise or negotiation with our enemy is flawed.

God protects us and surrounds us if we are seen as righteous in His eyes. Satan can request access to us, which is granted if God chooses to test our faithfulness.

The reverse is also true. I mentioned earlier that we have dominion over unclean spirits who are foot soldiers, but not over territorial spirits governing regions. There are situations where this can change.

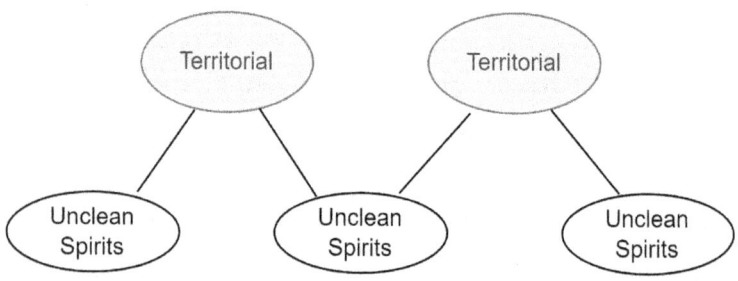

Figure 17.2 – Territorial Spirits over unclean spirits

We can approach God and ask for a strategy to take down a territorial spirit. My pastor needed council approval to build a new church. God revealed the territorial spirit that blocked the approval. This spirit was enormous in size and had an extremely terrifying appearance. God then gave the pastor a simple prayer as a means to bind the territorial spirit. "I can do all things through Christ who strengthens me". (Phil 4:13) A few months later, God provided another view of this territorial spirit. It was a wimpy little thing that could have been trodden on by accident. The council approved the building shortly after that.

## Preparing for the Battle

The battleground is found within the believer. His heart, his innermost being, is the battlefield on which the war is being fought. Preparation is key to being ready for the battle. That preparation requires discipline, education, and training in all types of warfare, as you never know what type of warfare you need to apply until the battle starts.

Just as a boxer doesn't take leave of conditioning for a fight by eating gourmet cakes and a soldier does not go to boot camp merely to enjoy camping next to tranquil streams, so we need to prepare for the battle.

## *Assess Yourself*

The first step in preparing is assessing whether there is any sin in your life. Anything that separates you from God will impede your progress. If you know of any outstanding sin, now is the time to repent of that and get back into a right relationship with God.

The second step is to get **Out of the Box**. In chapter five, I covered spiritual blindness, being **In the Box** versus **Out of the Box**. We are **In the Box** whenever we are self-focused. You can't fight this battle from within the box. When we are **In the Box**, people become the enemy, not Satan. Make every effort, each day, to stay **Out of the Box**.

The third step is to purge your negative thoughts. "As you think so you become." Positive thought processes are the foundation for building faith, not negativity.

The fourth step addresses pride. Pride inhibits us from seeing clearly and making the right decisions. Pride and arrogance lead us to trust in our own abilities and promote independence, rather than dependence on God. At this point, we are self-deluded and well-positioned to fail.

Finally, being Holy and sanctified positions you for God to move in your life. The closer you get to the Son, the better you will see.

## *Team up with the right people*

The greatest weakness in any church is the presence of those who are not faithful and lack a relationship with God. The greatest threat to Satan is a Christian who won't quit.

There is strength in attacking in one accord, in unity. However, a divided attack will fail. Obeying and not questioning leadership is one way to fight in unity and is pleasing to God. Work towards your leaders' vision and not your own.

Be careful who you let speak into your life. That person should be full of Godly wisdom. Teaming up with the wrong people with a vision that doesn't align with God's will is destined for disaster.

## *Partnership with God*

Seeking the Lord for wisdom and guidance before confronting an enemy is always a good start. It's essential to partner with God in all things. If you've achieved a victory, don't assume you'll have the same outcome next time. You may need a different approach next time.

A fitting word from God can be the key to turning a situation around. Spiritual discernment is needed to ensure that the instructions are from God to fulfil God's purposes.

If things don't go as expected, don't blame God. It may be that you've been deceived, or that you are out of step with God. To partner with God, you shouldn't act without Him, you shouldn't go ahead of Him, and you shouldn't trail behind Him.

Partnering with God means asking for the right strategy and approach.

## *The Right Strategy*

In physical warfare, timing and terrain are essential considerations. The type of terrain dictates the appropriate form of warfare. Selecting the right kind of warfare is crucial for success, with timing following closely behind. When is the optimal moment to attack, in the most effective manner? Remember, Satan uses this approach against you.

Some strategies require intercession, sometimes involving fasting. Occasionally, it's a simple prayer; at other times, it may not be. Often, it's merely an act of kindness that unlocks a door, providing an opportunity to share Christ.

For every battle, there is a strategy that leads to victory. Strategies from God are always a sure winner. Intelligence on the enemy always provides the upper hand. Seek God for this intel.

In every battle, and with every victory, give glory to God. Entertaining thoughts that you did it and that you're wonderful is a foothold for pride, and you might find yourself without help from the Almighty in the next battle. Don't fall victim to self.

## ON THE FRONT FOOT

On the front foot means to be in a dominant or advantageous position, to take the initiative, and to act assertively.

## *Seeking God*

God often has an agenda we do not know about, and from our perspective, we only see conflict and adversity. Seek God for a strategy and His perspective on a situation. His ways are higher than our ways; His thoughts are higher than our thoughts.

In physical combat, some weapons offer an advantage on the plains, while others are better suited for the hills. Some strategies are effective on the plains, while others are more appropriate for hilly terrain. For every situation, there exists a weapon and a strategy. Similarly, in Spiritual Warfare, seeking God for the right approach and the right resources is akin to sharpening the axe before chopping the tree. He that sharpens the axe is wise.

Sometimes, God gives us something seemingly small to do, or just one person to witness to who appears to be a closed book. However, that one person could hold the key to a multitude. We don't see the whole picture. Just because you've been given a small task does not mean it's a small or insignificant outcome.

Consider helping in the kids' church. Few people outside of the immediate parents volunteer for this. But each of those little individuals will grow up. If they grow up in Christ and you've helped in kids' church, how great is that impact?

The Battle may require decisive, ad-hoc decisions to be made as events unfold. This means current plans need to be flexible and open to change as situations and events dictate. God doesn't always give you all the facts up front. In that way, you are even more reliant on Him for direction.

## *Declarations*

We can read his promises out aloud back to God in his word. We can also read them out aloud to ourselves. We need to hear them spoken by our own lips into our own unbelieving ears. In time, their living impact will set our souls on fire with the assurance of what we already are and have by simple faith in Christ.

## *Worship*

Worship is a greatly underestimated weapon in our arsenal. It has the power to shift the atmosphere and chase off any lingering demons. In the midst of battle, it directs your attention away from yourself and your circumstances and toward the living God. Your focus will move from the problem to the solution. Worship will revive your soul.

## *Intercession*

Intercession is another great avenue for taking ground. Chapter twenty-two is dedicated to this, but I want to make a brief reference to it in the context of the battle.

Intercession is greatly underestimated in the church. Prayer underpins God's moving in a situation. This is best done with a prayer partner or prayer group:

> *For where two or three gather in my name, there am I with them.* (Matt 18:19)

Worship and giving thanks are always good ways to begin intercessory prayer. Don't approach God with a wish list. Enter His gates with thanksgiving and His courts with praise.

Now ask whatever it is in His name. Is anything too difficult for the Almighty? If there is, then He's not almighty.

## *Evangelism*

Just as great military commanders at times needed to be creative in their strategies, so do we. If someone isn't open to the gospel, maybe you just need a new creative approach.

Do not think you need to evangelise everyone in your office or on the street. It is better to focus on just two or three individuals and build bridges to them. Form a quality relationship by getting to know that person. People always want to talk about themselves, so getting to know someone shouldn't be difficult. However, there are those who don't open up about themselves, but I've found that perseverance usually leads to a breakthrough.

As you get to know your new friend, you are building intel. This intel forms the basis for intercessory prayer. For example, asking them about their interests and activities will often reveal if they are drawn to anything new age. If so, through intercession, you can break those demonic forces off their life. What's their worldview? Do they hold any Christian values? Pray that God will open their eyes and their understanding to see the truth.

Armed with intel and having broken demonic bondage from your friend, it's time to ask God for the opportunity to share your faith. That is, if you haven't had that opportunity already.

Remember, if the weather washes away the bridge, build a stronger one. Learn from what works and what does not work in every failed initiative. Quitters never win, and winners never quit.

## On the Back Foot

On the back foot means to be out-maneuvered by the enemy and be at a disadvantage.

After you've successfully taken ground, the enemy will immediately come to rob, kill, and destroy. On that day, you will need to transfer your fighting from the front foot to the back foot. You need to stand and stand firm, having put on the whole armour of God.

## *Our Enemy shows no mercy*

Our enemy shows no mercy, cannot be negotiated with, and pre-empts attacks. He lures you into ambushes. He strikes from multiple sides, and when you least expect it.

## *Indirect Attacks*

He will employ indirect attacks by targeting someone close to you, either by causing physical illness or by manipulating someone near you to launch his strikes, and those strikes will hurt even more when they come from someone you love.

An indirect attack is always meant to take your attention from the real issue. In this case, don't react; respond. Don't engage in the emotions of the moment at hand, as it is important to maintain self-control, look at the situation rationally, and then ask God for the root cause of this attack and how that root cause can be neutralized.

## *The Real Fight*

The real fight is behind the scenes, for we are not content with flesh and blood, principalities, and powers. We need to understand that the people screaming at us are not our true adversaries; instead, it is the spirit operating through them that is.

Once you identify the root cause, take authority in the name of Jesus and bind that tormenting spirit. Remind those spirits that they are a defeated foe and have no future. You are a child of God and have inherited the authority of Christ; therefore, they must go.

## *More than a Conqueror*

Remember this: there have been numerous times when Israel faced overwhelming odds and emerged victorious. Do you recall the story of Gideon? Three hundred Israelites stood against one hundred and thirty-five thousand Midianites. God granted Gideon the victory. In another battle, an angel of the Lord struck down one hundred and eighty-five thousand Assyrians. If God is on your side, that constitutes a majority in any battle.

*In all things, you are more than a conqueror through Christ, who strengthens you.* (Rom 8:37)

## FALLBACK AND REGROUP

There is a time to charge the enemy, a time to stand your ground, and a time to retreat when the battle is overwhelming. Falling back and regrouping is not cowardice; it is a way to return to the battle once you've regained your strength. Live to fight another day.

Fight your battles one at a time to avoid being overwhelmed. Losing a single battle does not end the war. It is better to lose a battle, fall back, and regroup than to completely give up.

Satan attacks us and orchestrates situations to compel us to betray or abandon our God, sometimes under the threat of losing our own lives. If the attack has escalated to the point where your life or the lives of your loved ones are threatened, it might be time to fall back and regroup.

Satan's overwhelming attack from multiple directions is designed to push you to the brink of giving up, not just the battle but Christ Himself. Falling back does not mean giving up on Christ; rather, it is a pause in your participation in the battle to regain your strength. This is not a coward's way out; it is a means of holding on to Christ to gather your strength so that you can engage in the battle at a more opportune time.

Realize that this is the tactic your enemy uses. He will attack you, and when you resist the devil, he will flee. However, he then returns at a more opportune time. Therefore, we should too. There comes a time when it is appropriate to take a break from the battle.

That doesn't mean taking a break from the church or stopping your quiet time with God. On the contrary, you need church, fellowship, and meditation on the Word of God as the keys to reviving your spirit. Just as King David strengthened himself in the Lord at Ziglag.

Once your spirit is revived and your strength returned, you will be able to see clearly again and be in a position to seek God for the next step.

## Spiritual Mapping

Spiritual Mapping is a tool that involves researching and identifying spiritual influences over specific regions or groups of people.

Now that you are armed with knowledge of the enemy hierarchy, you can apply it through spiritual mapping. Spiritual mapping involves identifying the demonic spirits over a city or region that are blinding the unchurched to the good news of the gospel.

Spiritual Mapping has a close relationship to intercession and discernment

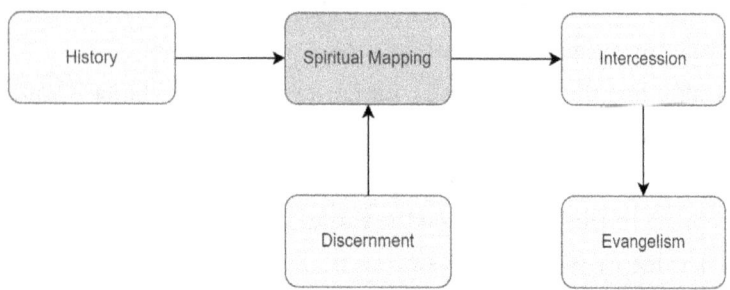

Figure 17.3 – Spiritual Mapping Underpins Evangelism

The basic approach involves three teams. The first group researches the history of the city or region. The second seeks God for divine insight into the territorial spirits that have dominion over the area. Once all data, both physical and spiritual, have been compiled, the third group reviews the information, comparing the two for accuracy. This third group then seeks God for a strategy on how to disempower and evict the territorial spirits. [38]

It is important to note that this should not be done in isolation. The best results come from engaging local churches in unity, followed by evangelism, where all the local churches are involved.

Expect a reasonable amount of attack and opposition when engaging in spiritual warfare at this level.

I can strongly recommend "Breaking Spiritual Strongholds in Your City" by C. Peter Wagner, for those who want a deep dive into this subject. In his books, he takes several different examples of approaches that pastors have used successfully.

# Footholds

A foothold is a military term referring to a secure position from which further progress can be made. A foothold of the enemy is not the end of the battle. It's the beginning. If you give the devil a foothold, he will use it to launch further attacks.

## PROGRESSION OF EVIL

Sin usually begins as a thought, a desire of some kind that is self-seeking. As you entertain that thought or desire, like any meditation, it impacts your heart and becomes a foothold.

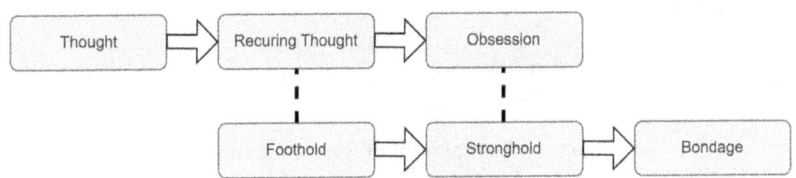

Figure 18.1 - Progressive attack

A foothold becomes a secure position for a deeper invasion, a stronghold. The final state is bondage.

Paul in Ephesians writes:

> *Do not let the sun go down while you are still angry, and do not give the devil a foothold (Eph 4:26)*

It is at the point of foothold that the devil has an opportunity to attack and ensure your thoughts continue so that sin is made manifest. Throughout much of this book, I've mentioned meditation as meditating on the Word of God. The thoughts you entertain influence your heart and impact your emotions. When you meditate on the Word of God, you begin to adopt the mind of Christ, becoming the hands and feet of Christ. Conversely, when you focus on your own selfish desires, it takes you away from Christ, making you more like Satan.

I refer to the foothold as the first state and the stronghold as the second state. If these thought patterns are not disrupted, they lead to the third state: bondage. Once you enter the third state, you can't break free on your own. You need help from someone you can be held accountable to, like a church leader or pastor. The best scenario is to stop the recurring thought at the foothold stage before the desire takes hold and the devil gets involved.

Let's see how this plays out in terms of pornography.

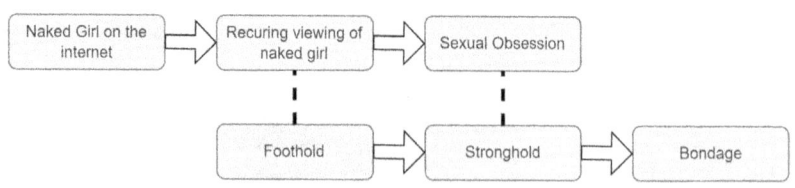

Figure 18.2 – Spiritual progression example

Imagine, while surfing the internet, you accidentally click something, and a picture of a naked woman appears. You could click the back button and think nothing more of it. But instead, you click the image to get to the website that's full of naked women. At this point, you've entered stage one, the foothold. The next day, being fed by the lusts of the devil, you return to the website. Pornography has started to become an obsession. You are starting to enter stage two, the stronghold. This pattern may keep recurring for weeks as you think you can stop whenever you want. But you won't know when you've progressed to stage three, bondage, until you try and break free and can't.

I am using pornography as an example, as it is a common problem in the church today. However, the principle applies to many different areas. Pornography is particularly harmful, as many of those who enter stage three either aren't aware of it or are too embarrassed to seek help. If you are one of these people and you've entered stage two, then make yourself accountable to someone. If this has been going on for a long time, then you have likely entered stage three, and you need to seek professional help.

## FOOTHOLDS THE DEVIL EXPLOITS

The footholds the devil will use to exploit you are tied up in the weaknesses of man. We all have one or more of these weaknesses active in our lives. These weaknesses all have their basis in selfishness.

### *Selfishness*

Selfishness revolves around feeding our selfish desires and indulging in pleasures that compromise our moral standards. It underpins all the other weaknesses of man: anger, fear, laziness, lust, greed, self-righteousness, and vanity.

Figure 18.3 – Weaknesses of Man

## *Anger*

Anger, like many of our emotions, is a gift from God. A gift that can be used positively or negatively. There is a righteous anger that rises up when we see injustice, but when unrighteous anger arises, it becomes a foothold for the devil.

There are numerous causes for anger. Some are psychological, some biological, and some social.

**Psychological Causes of Anger:**

- Unmet Expectations – When reality doesn't match what you expected.

- Feeling Disrespected – Perceived insults, rejection, or unfair treatment.
- Frustration – Obstacles preventing you from achieving a goal.
- Past Trauma – Old wounds resurfacing due to triggers.
- Feeling Powerless – Lack of control in a situation.

**Biological Causes of Anger:**

- Brain Chemistry – Imbalances in neurotransmitters (like serotonin) can affect mood.
- Hormones – Stress hormones like cortisol and adrenaline can increase irritability.
- Sleep Deprivation – Lack of rest can lower patience and self-control.
- Hunger – Low blood sugar can make you more irritable.

**Social & Environmental Causes of Anger:**

- Stress – Work, finances, relationships, or life challenges.
- Cultural Norms – Some environments encourage aggression or suppress emotions, leading to bottled-up anger.
- Peer Influence – Being around angry or aggressive people can normalize the behaviour.

**Cognitive Causes of Anger:**

- Negative Thinking Patterns – Jumping to conclusions, black-and-white thinking, or catastrophising.
- Feeling Misunderstood – Not being heard or valued in conversations.
- Perceived Injustice – Seeing something as unfair or morally wrong.

We need to make every effort to:

> *Be Angry and don't sin; do not let the sun go down on your wrath, nor give place to the devil.* (Eph 4:26-27)

Notice the bible doesn't say don't be angry, but be angry and don't sin. In other words, don't entertain this emotion as it gives a foothold for the devil.

The key to overcoming this behaviour is self-control. Stop anger before it becomes rage. At the point of rage, you have completely lost control. If you are spirit-filled, then self-control is one of the fruits of the Spirit. Praying in tongues will help aid your self-control. If you work long hours and experience a lack of sleep, this will deplete your self-control.

Exercise, especially after work, can be a great outlet for emotions like anger and often leads to restful sleep, which also aids in coping with stress and anger derived from current circumstances.

## *Fear*

This emotion is disempowering. The Bible encourages us to fear God and not man. But most of us have this back to front, we fear man and not God. This ideology is stupid. If God made us, can He not unmake us? As Jesus said, man can take your life, but can do nothing more to you. When it comes to fear, our view of the world is flawed.

Did you know that ninety percent of all news feeds and social media stories are negative? This negativity feeds our fear and anxiety. Just in case you manage to overcome your fears and anxieties, the world is here to help. It keeps you feeling anxious all over again.

Then there is our great adversary, the devil. He doesn't want you to witness to the lost or encourage fellow believers. In fact, he will oppose any activity that furthers the kingdom of God. So, be encouraged when you see him on your case; you know you're on to something.

It's a small wonder that we all need the peace of God that surpasses all understanding. In that place of God's peace, it doesn't matter what is happening around you; you have inner peace and an inner knowing that it will all be alright.

Being filled with fear and anxiety really boils down to what you believe about yourself and the world around you. If you believe every news article, your anxiety level will increase. If you believe you are going to be made redundant at work, your anxiety will increase. If you believe you will be ridiculed for your faith if you witness to someone, then you won't reach out to the lost. You will isolate yourself to avoid pain and suffering. It is in our nature to move away from pain and suffering and towards pleasure. This is not what Jesus did. He is the true representation of how we should live our lives.

Fear is a key weapon of the devil to ensure you remain ineffective as a Christian. This battle is one you must fight and win. It begins by stepping back from the emotion. Rather than letting your emotions lead you, allow your spirit to take charge. Start introducing yourself to the fearful situation gradually. Fear will arise, but since you are addressing this little by little, the level of fear won't be overwhelming. Your spirit should take the lead. In this approach, you confront your fears instead of running away from them.

I used to have an intense fear of public speaking. If I was in a group of more than four people, I would stay silent, unable to utter a word. I joined Toastmasters, where I had the opportunity to speak in a controlled and safe environment. Slowly, over time, I gained more confidence. Later, this small victory became important when I joined IBM and had to run training courses—courses that, at first, did not go well. However, over time, I gained even more confidence, and my anxieties diminished.

## *Laziness*

*As a door turns on its hinges, so does the lazy man on his bed.* (Prov 26:14)

For a long time, I watched Netflix as a way to unwind. Sometimes for several hours a day, on most days. I gained weight, began to feel lethargic, and became a couch potato. Then, two things began to occur around the same time. I started to struggle to find anything I could consider entertaining. The Holy Spirit also began to convict me that I was wasting time—time that could be used for something productive.

Jesus, in Matthew 25:14, tells the parable of the ten talents. Three servants are given talents: one receives five talents, another receives two talents, and the last one gets one talent. The first two servants invest the money and earn a profit from their labour. The master is pleased with them. However, the last servant buried his talent and has no profit to show for it. Verse thirty reveals what Jesus thought about the unprofitable servant:

> *Cast the worthless servant into the outer darkness. In that place there will be weeping and gnashing of teeth.* (Matt 25:30)

In the times we live in (End Times) we can't afford to be unprofitable. Time and money are the only two resources you have to invest in the kingdom of God. This is your time in the Earth. Make the most of it.

## *Lust*

To admire someone of the opposite sex as being attractive is not evil; it's natural. It's when the desire to have sex with the individual comes onto the screen of your mind that you create a foothold the devil can exploit.

The strength of this foothold will vary from person to person and is strongest during adolescence. As with all footholds, you need to change your thinking before it progresses to a stronghold. Lust is a very powerful force, which in the context of marriage is very beautiful, and incredibly destructive outside of marriage.

The key you will need is self-control over your thoughts to change your thinking before it takes hold. Self-control is one of the fruits of the Spirit. If you are spirit-filled, this is the time to pray in tongues.

Make every effort to stop this while it is still a foothold. Once it becomes a stronghold, it will only take a small amount of self-delusion for you to end up in bondage.

## *Greed*

> *Hell, and Destruction are never full; so the eyes of man are never satisfied.* (Prov 27:20)

Greed is all about feeding our selfish desires. The more we have, the more we want. The eye is never satisfied. Like any other evil intent, the more you feed it, the more it grows.

Gluttony is a specific kind of greed related to eating. The principle remains the same, as both denote an excessive desire for more than is necessary.

If left unchecked, gluttony can lead to obesity, while greed leads to vanity, self-absorption, and self-idolatry.

The key to breaking this is knowing when it is enough. When you eat, you eat to fuel your body. That doesn't necessarily mean filling your stomach. If you are used to overeating, your stomach will be stretched, and you will need to eat more food than you need to feel satisfied.

Start eating less food, and after a while, your stomach will shrink, allowing you to feel satisfied with smaller portions. You are no longer a glutton, and you are only eating what you need.

Likewise, you need certain possessions to live as God intended you to live. You likely need a car. Does it have to be a new car? Does it have to be a new Porsche? Are possessions ruling you, or are you ruling possessions? You can break out of this by stopping being greedy and starting to be conservative. It will be difficult at first, but as you think less about yourself and more about God and the kingdom of God, the right choices will become much clearer and easier.

## *Self-Righteousness*

Self-righteousness is the belief that you are more moral and virtuous than others. It is closely related to self-comparison, with judgment following closely behind. When you compare your morals to someone else's, you will view that person as either superior or inferior. Both perspectives require judgment to arrive at a conclusion. This mindset can become a foothold for jealousy.

Stop judging others and stop comparing yourself with others, is the beginning of stopping self-righteousness.

> *For all have sinned and fallen short of the glory of God* (Rom 3:23)

We are saved by grace and not by works. No one is able to save him or herself through self-righteousness. To think you can is self-deluded.

## *Vanity*

*Pride goes before destruction* (Prov 16:18)

This is the most dangerous weakness of man. Satan's fall can be traced back to vanity. Vanity begins with a God-given gift, a talent at which you excel. You may receive some honour and glory for your God-given talent, and then self-pride kicks in, leading you to think more highly of yourself than is appropriate. You become self-deluded. This is how Satan fell.

> *I will ascend into heaven, I will exalt my throne above the stars of God; I will also sit on the mount of the congregation, On the farthest sides of the north; I will ascend above the heights of the clouds, I will be like the Most High* (Isaiah 14:12-14)

He was the worship leader in heaven. He received honour and glory, and it all went to his head. He became so deluded that he saw himself as equal to God.

This type of delusion can lead to spiritual blindness, a foothold the devil loves to exploit, as you remain unaware of the fact that you have a problem.

People suffering from this weakness are not people with strong self-esteem, but weak self-esteem.

To break free, be vigilant in monitoring your thought patterns. When you see a vain thought rise up, stop it. Recognize it as a distorted view of the world. Remember, you are created by God, for God, and if you do anything wonderful, give glory to God. In all circumstances, seek to be humble. Next, find scriptures about the love of God and meditate on these.

## *Scriptures for Humility*

> *Be completely humble and gentle; be patient, bearing with one another in love.* (Eph 4:2)

# THE DEFINITIVE GUIDE TO SPIRITUAL WARFARE

> *God opposes the proud but shows favour to the humble.*
> (James 4:6)

> *But you are a chosen generation, a royal priesthood, a holy nation, His own people, that you may proclaim the praises of Him who called you out of darkness into His Marvelous light.*
> (1 Peter 2:9)

## The Inner Critic

Our thought patterns fall into one of four categories: Critical Parent, Nurturing Parent, Adaptive Child, and Rebellious Child. This is also known in psychology as transactional analysis. These patterns of thinking have been learned from our parents. As parents, we tend to reproduce after ourselves.

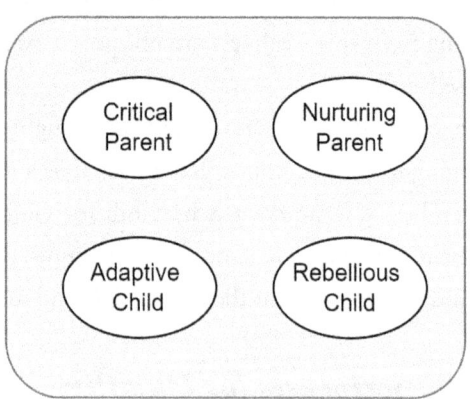

Figure 18.4 - Personas of Thinking

## *Nurturing Parent*

The Nurturing Parent reflects the positive influences of caregivers, mentors, and role models. In this mindset, you exhibit nurturing, advising, and protecting.

## *Critical Parent*

The Critical Parent represents the negative influences of authority figures that lead to criticism, judgment, and control over oneself and others.

## *Adaptive Child*

The Adaptive Child represents behaviours and emotions that were acceptable to caregivers during childhood. This is where the child learns to comply with authorities.

## *Rebellious Child*

The Rebellious Child represents behaviours and emotions that were discouraged in childhood. This is where the child does not comply with the authorities.[35]

## *Foothold of the Inner Critic*

A healthy mind will have all four types of thinking active at different times. Problems occur when the rebellious child thinking becomes predominant, which can lead to laziness. If the critical parent thinking is too dominant, you may beat yourself up for the smallest shortcomings. This creates a significant foothold, giving rise to condemnation, self-rejection, and a distorted view of God. Individuals with an overly critical parent often struggle to believe that God can forgive them, leading to their inability to forgive themselves.

## Destroying Footholds

Regardless of the foothold, it needs to be destroyed before it becomes a stronghold. This involves capturing the wrong thinking before a foothold is established and changing the thought to align with the Word of God.

*Casting down arguments and every high thing that exalts itself against the knowledge of God, bringing every thought into captivity to the obedience of Christ* (2 Cor 10:5)

This means replacing your negative thoughts with something positive. It's even better if you can declare a scripture in the situation that inspires faith and hope.

## *Declaration Scriptures*

*Finally, brethren, whatever things are true, whatever things are noble, whatever things are just, whatever things are pure, whatever things are lovely, whatever things are of good report, if there is any virtue and if there is anything praiseworthy—meditate on these things* (Phil 4:8)

*But you are a chosen generation, a royal priesthood, a holy nation, His own people, that you may proclaim the praises of Him who called you out of darkness into His Marvelous light.* (1 Peter 2;9)

*Yet in all these things we are more than conquerors through Him who loved us.* (Rom 8:37)

*"The Lord your God is with you, the Mighty Warrior who saves. He will take great delight in you; in his love he will*

*no longer rebuke you, but will rejoice over you with singing."* (Zep 3:17)

*For I know the plans I have for you,"* declares the Lord, *"plans to prosper you and not to harm you, plans to give you hope and a future.* (Jer 29:11)

# Stronghold

A stronghold can be defined as a significant, established occupancy of an enemy.
By definition, a stronghold in a Christian's life can be any part of your life where the devil has invaded and robbed, killed or destroyed.

> *The thief does not come except to steal and to kill, and to destroy. (John 10:10)*

In the previous chapter, we covered footholds and open doors through which the devil gains access. Once he has a foothold, he will use it to establish a more significant position, a stronghold. That little indiscretion that you thought you could do just once or twice has developed into a recurring habit.

Any of the weaknesses of man: anger, fear, laziness, lust, greed, self-righteousness, or vanity can be used to transition to a stronghold.

The devil builds strongholds that eventually become bondages. By the time the invasion has reached the bondage stage, you need to seek professional help to break free. That help can come from a pastor, psychologist, counsellor, or support person.

As strongholds and bondage are very closely related, both will be covered in this chapter.

## A Multi-Dimensional Problem

Strongholds can occur in any area of your life, not just your mind and spirit. I have identified the following areas where the enemy can create a stronghold.

Stronghold Dimensions:

- Spiritual
- Emotional
- Mental
- Physical
- Financial

A stronghold can be multi-dimensional. A physical addiction can, and often does, exist due to mental or spiritual issues. Financial challenges can contribute to mental and emotional problems.

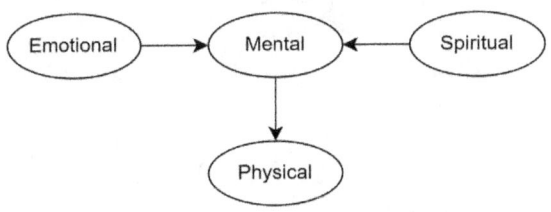

Figure 19.1 - Stronghold of addiction

In the illustration above, drug addiction has developed as a means of relief from mental issues such as depression. The state of depression is fuelled by emotions and spiritual attacks from the enemy in our minds to reinforce the depression.

If the addiction is treated in isolation, then relief is only temporary. The underlying issue driving the addiction must be treated first.

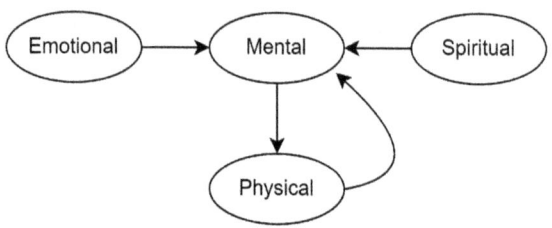

Figure 19.2 – Long-term addiction

A variation of the addiction stronghold occurs when the mind is damaged from repeated use of drugs and/or alcohol, and the victim can no longer function cognitively. In other words, they cannot control their thought processes, and their ability to combat the addiction is significantly compromised.

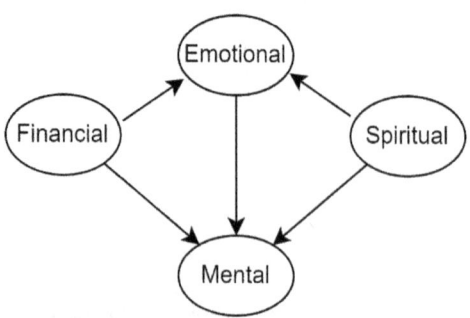

Figure 19.3 – Strongholds causing depression

In this scenario, multiple issues drive the mental stronghold. Lack of finances creates emotional and mental stress. The devil plants thoughts and situations to further increase your stress and reinforce your mental stronghold.

You can see a spider's web forming where multiple areas of your life are manipulated by the devil working together for a specific purpose.

The release from the stronghold must consider other contributing dimensions. In the case of depression, breaking strongholds of finance and spiritual forces should be addressed before the mental and emotional aspects.

It is beyond the scope of this book to cover every dimension of strongholds, so I will focus on the most common, starting with spiritual strongholds.

## Spiritual Strongholds

A spiritual stronghold often manifests as demonic oppression, usually due to an open door to the demonic realm. Spiritual bondage represents a final state where the individual is either demon-possessed and cannot escape without help from a deliverance ministry, or they are bound to habitual sin.

There are numerous pathways to spiritual strongholds. In each case, the journey starts with a foothold—a seemingly insignificant beginning into something new. As with most new experiences, it can be exciting. The new doctrine can sound so right and feel so good. Like a sugar-coated arsenic pill, it tastes so sweet, it feels so good, and it will kill you, like it almost killed me.

Much of the new age movement is like this. The diagram below gives some insight into the different pathways to spiritual strongholds.

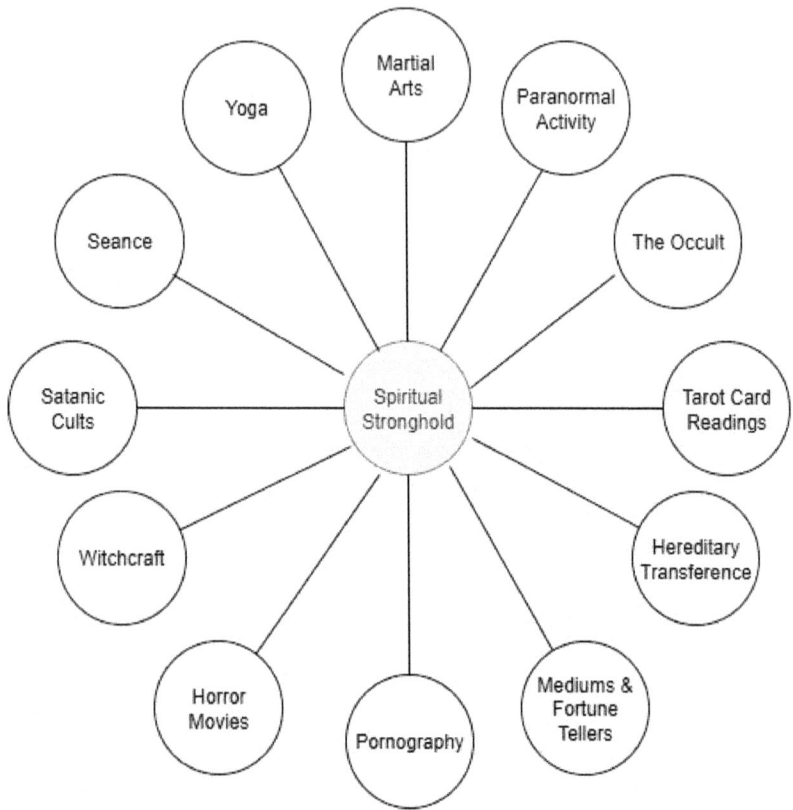

Figure 19.4 – Pathways to spiritual strongholds

My journey into martial arts has taught me a great deal about the spiritual realm. Many forms of yoga and martial arts are physical in nature, and the exercise is beneficial. However, once you introduce Eastern meditation, you enter the spiritual side of these systems. In martial arts, it often begins with a simple Buddhist meditation, and that marks the start of your demonic oppression. In most cases, the spiritual invasion is gradual unless the victim progresses to a more advanced form of meditation.

# STRONGHOLDS

Yoga also starts with simple meditation that takes a long time to have a significant effect. Advanced yoga meditation, in particular Kundalini Yoga, can have instant or near-instant effects, damaging you spiritually and mentally. As the Kundalini rises through the seven psychic centres, it reaches the brain where it biologically alters the brain structure, opening up telepathy and clairvoyance. If the energy force is polluted or misdirected, it will destroy brain cells, causing various forms of insanity, loss of bodily functions, and death. This is the devil's endgame.

The key takeaway is that the spiritual stronghold or demonization is a continuum. The longer you are exposed to these demonic influences, the further you will progress towards demon possession.

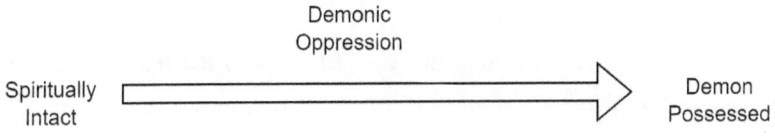

Figure 19.5 – Demonisation continuum

It is like a progressive sickness that starts with insignificant symptoms. The more it progresses, the more it controls your thoughts, emotions, and actions.

Irrespective of how the demonic oppression started, the solution is the same. Kick it out and close the door. Closing the door is just as important as kicking it out.

It is likely you will need to seek a skilled professional for this task. Someone who is experienced and works with others, as there should be multiple people present in prayer during any deliverance session. The people you seek out to help with deliverance need to be anointed for the task and have spiritual authority, or they may fail to deliver you in the first place. Most importantly, they need to close the door through which the demon gained access. As:

> When an unclean spirit goes out of a man, he goes through dry places, seeking rest, and finds none. Then he says, 'I will return to my house from which I came.' And when he comes, he finds it empty, swept, and put in order. 45 Then he goes and takes with him seven other spirits more wicked than himself, and they enter and dwell there; and the last state of that man is worse than the first. So shall it also be with this wicked generation (Matt 12:43-44)

## *After Care*

Once you're free, you must stay free. I have seen too many deliverance ministries completely overlook this. Aftercare is essential, not optional. It's the key to remaining free. Aftercare consists of worship, fellowship, and meditating on the Word of God; it's so simple that it is often overlooked. Worship will drive demons from your immediate environment. Fellowship with other believers who are like-minded and understand your journey is crucial. Lastly, daily meditation on the Word of God and letting it renew your heart and mind will help you to stay free.

## *Warning*

Casting a demon out of someone who doesn't have a demon is a traumatic experience. You could find yourself needing deliverance from the deliverance people.

## STRONGHOLDS OF THE MIND

Strongholds of the mind, in reality, cover every aspect of psychology and is a topic that could fill multitudes of books. A stronghold of the mind can be any recurring pattern of thinking that is contradictory to the word of God. We all suffer from this to some degree.

*We demolish arguments and every pretension that sets itself up against the knowledge of God, and we take captive every thought to make it obedient to Christ.* (2 Cor 10:5)

During my research, I experienced a profound moment while reading a book on strongholds. At that moment, the Holy Spirit spoke to me about something entirely different. He revealed to me the mental images of the structures that the devil creates through various events in our lives, which hinder us from being the effective soldiers of Christ that God intended us to be. What follows are the structures that were revealed to me, along with the strategies to dismantle the works of the enemy.

## STRUCTURES

There are primarily three structures (these are not the only structures) that the devil builds to keep you bound.
- Low Self-Esteem
- Wrong Core Beliefs
- Trauma

These three, once constructed, interact to keep you bound. All the devil needs to do is ensure there is enough affliction in your life to prevent you from breaking these structures. Let me tell you straight: it's time to smash open these structures. The devil's reign is over.

## STRUCTURE OF LOW SELF-ESTEEM

Low self-esteem is the root cause of many seemingly trivial sins, the most significant of which is vanity. Your mind uses vain thoughts to compensate for low self-esteem, not because you possess high self-esteem. Low self-esteem undermines your confidence in your ability to act, disempowering you from being all that Christ wants you to be.

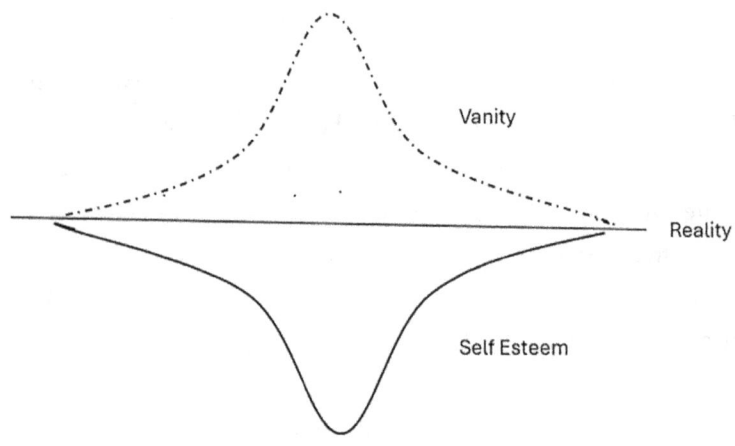

Figure 19.6 – Low self-esteem compensated by vanity

In this structure, your mind compensates for low self-esteem by entertaining vain thoughts. The vain thoughts in turn push God away when in fact you need Him close, as He is your fortress and your strength.

It's time to smash open this stronghold. Below is a list of six scriptures to meditate on that will reprogram your heart and mind with the truth of who you are in Christ. A royal priesthood.

Don't rush this meditation; instead, set aside ten to twenty minutes each day. You might also consider reading the previous and next verses of the selected passage. Reflect deeply on the implications of what the Word of God conveys. How does that relate to you? Does it seem like the author is speaking about someone else? If you are in Christ, then he's addressing YOU, a royal priest, chosen by God before the beginning of time. YOU possess intrinsic value beyond measure. How do I know this? Jesus Christ and Him crucified, for YOU.

> *Blessed be the God and Father of our Lord Jesus Christ, who has blessed us with every spiritual blessing in the heavenly places in Christ, just as He chose us in him before the foundation of the world, that we should be holy and without blame before him, In love having predestined us for adoption as sons by Jesus Christ, according to the purpose of his will.*
> (Eph 1:3-5)

You have been blessed with every spiritual blessing, chosen before the beginning of the world for His special purpose, which He lovingly planned for you before time began. You are meant to be holy and blameless, adopted into God's own family. If you're adopted, you are not left alone or to your own devices; instead, you are in fellowship with God's family. As an adopted son or daughter, you have an inheritance that will not pass away or be given to another. You are truly blessed.

> *But you are a chosen generation, a royal priesthood, a holy nation, His own people, that you may proclaim the praises of Him who called you out of darkness into His Marvelous light.*
> (1 Peter 2:9)

You were chosen out of the world. Redeemed from destruction. Forgiven. Destined to live life eternal. A royal priest. A prince or princess and a priest of God. Holy and righteous in His sight. His own. You now belong to God, who called you out of the darkness into His light, a light that not only shines but also gives you everlasting life.

> *You did not choose me, but I chose you and appointed you that you should go and bear fruit and that your fruit should abide, so that whatever you ask the Father in my name, he may give it to you* (John 15:16)

He chose you. Of all the people He could have chosen, He chose you. Have you ever thought there were better people He could have chosen? People who are more attractive, smarter, younger, and more personable. But no, He chose you and has not cast you off or forsaken you.

> *'For I know the plans I have for you,' declares the Lord, 'plans to prosper you and not to harm you, plans to give you hope and a future."* (Jer 29:11)

He has plans for you—plans to bless you, to love you, to care for you. If God has a plan for you, then it's not a maybe; it's a certainty that will come to pass. If God's plans are to cause you to prosper, how great are those plans? What great things will they achieve in your life?

> *You whom I have taken from the ends of the earth, and called from its farthest regions, and said to you, 'You are My servant, I have chosen you and have not cast you away. So do not fear, for I am with you; do not be dismayed, for I am your God. I will strengthen you and help you; I will uphold you with my righteous right hand."* (Isa 41:9-10)

He has called you. From the farthest regions, He has called you. To be His servant. Whose servant? A servant of the Most High God. That's no small title. If you are a servant, you have duties and a purpose. You are not just fumbling through life. He has chosen you and has not cast you off. He hasn't changed His mind about you. He loves you just as much today as He did yesterday and the day before that. He is not going to stop loving you.

Therefore, fear not, for He who loves you is with you.

> *"The Lord your God is with you, the Mighty Warrior who saves. He will take great delight in you; in his love he will no longer rebuke you, but will rejoice over you with singing."* (Zep 3:17)

He, the Most High God, not only loves you but loves you enough to rejoice over you with singing. Just think about how much God must value you. He's not only in love with you but has written songs to sing over you. That's a deep love to write love songs.

You may have your own scriptures to meditate on that relate to who you are in Christ. Please don't limit yourself to those in this book.

By meditating on scripture and trying new things, you can build your self-esteem and overcome the psychological compensation of vanity. Engaging in activities like introductory scuba diving or speaking at Toastmasters, or anything that challenges you, can push you out of your comfort zone, allowing you to accomplish what you once thought was impossible. This transformation shifts you from a "can't do" person to a "can do" person, ultimately helping you grow your self-esteem.

Your self-esteem is closely linked to the core beliefs you develop about yourself and the world you live in. You will act out of what you believe. Wrong core beliefs are the next structure to smash open.

## STRUCTURE OF WRONG CORE BELIEFS

While we are young, the devil builds structures in our minds to form false beliefs that are contrary to the truth and will disempower us as believers. These are usually lies about who you are and what the world around you is. We tend to act out of what we believe, irrespective of whether that is right or wrong.

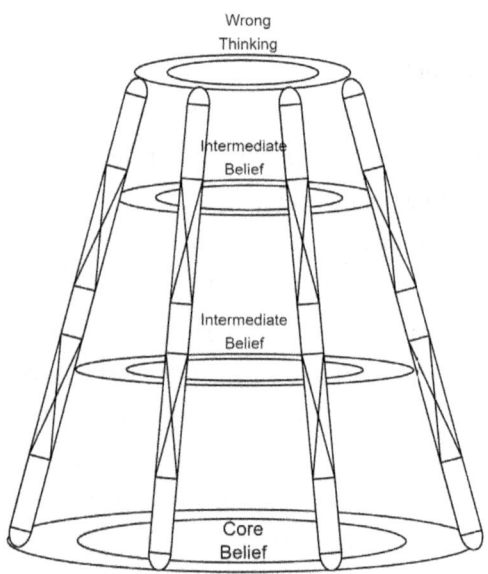

Figure 19.7 - Core Beliefs Planted by the Devil

The structure begins during your childhood with the devil introducing ideas like, "you're dumb," "you don't contribute," and "No one likes you." From that, you draw a conclusion: you are worthless. The core belief is worthlessness, the intermediate belief is that no one likes me, and I'm dumb. This leads to the idea that I'm not popular at work. This was me.

The devil used my parents to plant negative thoughts that became intermediate and core beliefs, which were lies. When the lie comes from someone you love, that hurts.

Some examples of Core Beliefs the Devil plants:

- I'm worthless
- I don't deserve love
- I'm unlovable
- I'm a failure
- I can't do anything right
- What's the use? Nothing is going to change

These may not be your core beliefs, but it's time to find out what is. In order to smash this stronghold, we need to first identify the core beliefs that have been built and have existed for most of our lives.[36]

This is best done with a Christian counselor who understands Cognitive Behavioral Therapy. They will get you over several weeks to fill in Negative Automatic Thought reports, which, when analysed, will help identify intermediate and core beliefs.

Of course you could buy a book on CBT and figure out how to do this without a counselor but your best results can be found by doing this with someone who can identify patterns in your thinking and will more accurately guide you to a core belief.

## Structure of Trauma

Trauma often underpins anger, anxiety, and depression, leading to trust issues. If your perpetrator was a primary caregiver who either neglected or betrayed you, the result can be poor relationships due to a lack of trust.

Whether you acknowledge it or not, and whether you remember it or not, the symptoms will manifest in your life somewhere.

Many counsellors and pastors describe a connection between trauma and spiritual oppression. This is only partly true. The traumatic incident itself does not expose you to the demonic realm. However, how you mentally process the event afterwards might. If your perpetrator is a primary caregiver, they have broken trust and hurt you, leading to unforgiveness, anger, resentment, and bitterness. Over time, this creates an opening for demonic influence that ensures the stronghold remains throughout your lifetime.

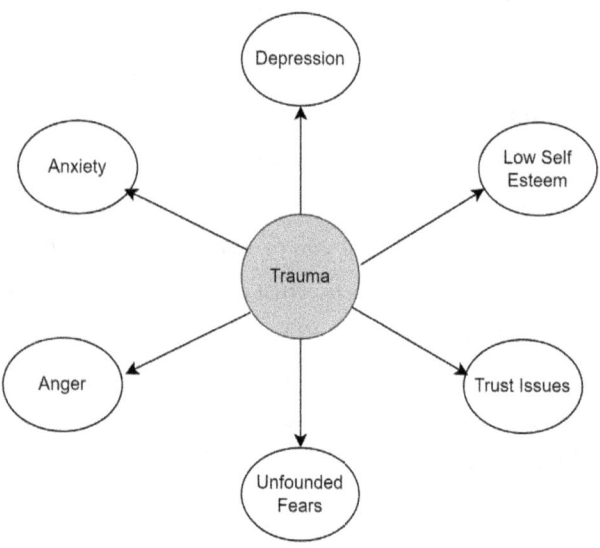

Figure 19.8 – Area's trauma affects

Satan uses early childhood trauma to create a different type of structure. He uses denial and repression to cover the trauma, thus ensuring the child never fully heals from the experience. The hurt is allowed to fester.

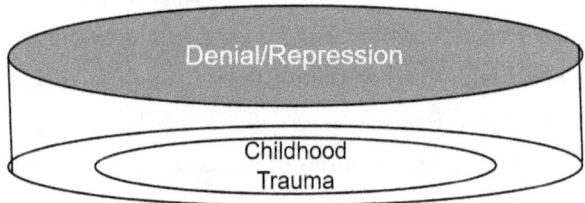

Figure 19.9 - Childhood trauma covered with denial or repression

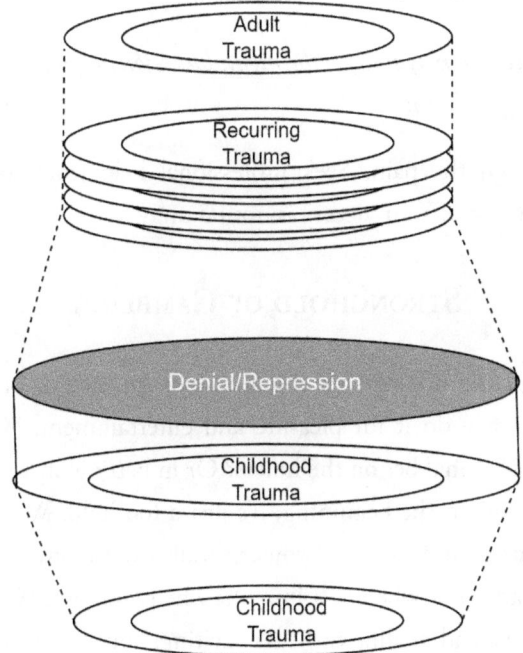

Figure 19.10 – Compounded trauma

The effects of childhood trauma propagate throughout your life, with the effects compounding one on top of the other, influencing teen and adult traumas.

Different traumas carry different impacts depending on the magnitude of the trauma and your reaction. Trauma experienced in childhood usually carries a greater magnitude than trauma faced in adulthood. The exception to this is the trauma of war.

The result is suppressed emotions of fear, anxiety, and anger that manifest unexpectedly and are used by Satan to destroy relationships. Only once denial is removed can healing take place, often with a counsellor. Revealing hidden childhood trauma can be painful. The wound may have been festering for decades. It will hurt to expose that which has been hidden.

> *Weeping may stay for the night, but rejoicing comes in the morning* (PS 30:5)

Push through the pain. Seek professional help from someone who specialises in trauma. Your victory is not far away.

## STRONGHOLD OF GAMBLING

Most people do not start gambling to gain an income or supplement their income; they do it for pleasure and entertainment. What harm is there in the occasional bet on the horses? Or in betting on your local football team to win? In the beginning, it's just a foothold. While it's a foothold, you aren't bound to it, and you can walk away at any time.

Problems arise not when you lose but when you win. When you win, you experience an adrenaline rush. It's exciting. Your life is no longer boring. This is reinforced by peer pressure to make another bet. Double or nothing. You end up walking away with nothing, but you come back next week with the prospect that you might win, and you can have that adrenaline hit all over again.

As the stronghold intensifies, you bet more money than you can afford to lose, and the stronghold consumes all you have to live on. The lack of money creates a desperation that reinforces the stronghold, as in your delusion, you think you can gamble your way out of debt.

If this is a stronghold in your life, you will need to make yourself accountable to someone you can call in your moment of weakness, such as a Church elder or pastor.

If you've reached the stage of bondage, then find a Gamblers Anonymous group before you lose more than just money. The devil has plans for you, not just to lose your money but your house, marriage, and family. Have you seen the homeless beggar on the street? He's not there because he's an evil person. He's there because he made the wrong choices. If gambling is your stronghold, escape starts with making the right choices.

## *The Game*

There's one variation of this stronghold I want to bring to your attention. I said in the beginning that most people don't start gambling to create a supplemental income. That's not completely true. With the increase in the cost of living and wages not rising to match, many people are turning to the share market to make short-term investments where a position in the market lasts anything from a few days to a few weeks. Charts with technical indicators are used to help determine the best stocks, when to buy, and when to sell. Some players of what I call "The Game" use sophisticated software that leverages AI to help pick the entry and exit points. The idea is to sell after making a small profit, and when this process is repeated, it becomes supplemental income.

The Game is a game of partly skill and partly luck. Those without skill are dependent on luck.

The Game takes on new powers when you progress to level two, leveraged products. Leveraged products are financial instruments over a financial asset, and they are leveraged. In other words, you can purchase a futures contract for one hundred ounces of gold at $3000 per ounce, with a one percent margin for just $3000 USD. (1% leverage. You aren't actually buying the gold but a contract for gold to be delivered. You control the equity.) You are then controlling $300,000 worth of gold. When it rises, you win; when it falls, you lose.

The more leveraged the financial asset, the shorter your time frame, the harder it is to play the game.

I played the game for many years, and it became a stronghold, as there was a hidden problem. Every time I took up a position in the market, it was a bet that the market would move in my favour. If I did this with any regularity, it started to become a hidden addiction. I stopped playing the game when I started to see technical indicators saying buy, only to see the stock fall the next day. This did not happen once or twice. It turned out that managed funds were manipulating the market, forcing it down while Mum and Dad investors thought it was going up, thereby taking from the poor and giving to the rich. The Game was rigged.

Be aware, there is a fine line between investing and gambling. The game may have a stronger hold on you than you think.

## STRONGHOLD OF ALCOHOL & DRUGS

I used to have a glass of wine after a hard day's work, as it instantly caused my brain to stop thinking about IT. A little wine, is good; a lot of wine is not good. The question you need to ask, with all honesty, is "Does wine rule me, or do I rule the wine?" Could I not drink for an entire month? If you can, then it's a stronghold you can tear down by limiting your drinking. If you can't, then you need to read on.

The physical stronghold of alcohol and drugs has been successfully dealt with by organizations like AA and NA using the 12-step approach.

These are the 12 Steps:

1. Honesty (Accepting there is a problem)
2. Faith (Faith in God)
3. Surrender (Give purpose)
4. Soul Searching (Inward reflection)
5. Integrity (Being honest and vulnerable)
6. Acceptance (Self-Esteem and letting go of the past)
7. Humility (Asking God for Help)
8. Willingness (Seek forgiveness from those offended or hurt)
9. Forgiveness (Forgiving those who have hurt or offended you)
10. Maintenance (Reviewing your progress)
11. Making Contact (Seeking God for your gifting & purpose)
12. Service (Applying what was learned to the rest of your life)

Considering steps seven, eight, and nine are most likely to break the mental strongholds that create the need for drugs and/or alcohol to mask inner pain. It is not surprising that they have a high degree of success.

Both Alcoholics Anonymous and Narcotics Anonymous offer free treatment, where you will receive a sponsor. They are highly effective, and there is a vast global network of support.

If you have reached the third state, the state of bondage, you will need help to break free. Don't hesitate to reach out for help.

- Alcoholics Anonymous: https://www.aa.org/
- Narcotics Anonymous: https://na.org/

## Stronghold of Lust

If you look at the top five issues facing the church today, lust is well within the top five. It's a stronghold for both men and women at all levels of the church.

Pornography is a significant driver of this stronghold, largely due to the internet. Most surveys conducted around 2012 reported that an average of thirty percent of internet traffic was pornographic. It is likely that this figure is much higher today.

I have been in IT for most of my life and there was a long period when porn websites targeted geeks. (They still do to a lesser extent) When you search for answers to technical problems, ads of semi-clothed women would pop up. Some were dating websites and others were porn sites. There was a day when I clicked on one of these and it took me to a porn site. At this point in the story, the enemy has a foothold. But I didn't close the browser and walk away as I should have. Within three days, I saw this grow from a foothold to a stronghold. When it takes hold, it is incredibly powerful.

This is something that needs to be stopped while it's a foothold. To entertain it to any degree is like feeding a bad dog. It will bite you.

It's time to smash this stronghold open with all you've got. The first step is to repent. Remember what the Bible says:

> *If we confess our sins, he is faithful and just and will forgive us our sins and purify us from all unrighteousness* (1 John 1:9)

Ask the Lord to forgive and cleanse you from all unrighteousness and heal your soul.

The second step is that if you have been in a relationship outside of marriage, then you need to break soul ties. When you are involved in sexual relations outside of marriage, there is a spiritual transference that occurs during sex. Within a marriage, the two become one flesh. This is God's design. Outside of marriage, you become defiled. If this is you, pray this declaration prayer: "I sever all spiritual ties and cast out all demonic spirits that have gained access through this sexual relationship. I renounce the works of the devil. I close the spiritual door that I have opened and close the door to any and all demonic influences, in Jesus name."

The third step is that if you've been exposed to porn, particularly on the internet, you will have opened the door to a spirit of lust. It's time to kick out that demonic squatter. Pray this prayer: "I come in the authority of Jesus Christ, as a child of the Most High God, and I command you, spirit of lust, to leave right now, never to return again. I close the door of pornography and sever all ties to the spirit of lust. Spirit of lust, begone in the name of Jesus."

The last step is to find someone to whom you can be accountable (pastor, friend, or small group leader). No, this is not an option. It's not time to wimp out. Next, you need to buy software that tracks and monitors the websites you visit. This will send an alert via email to whoever you made yourself accountable to.

No, don't just install this software on your laptop and then use your phone to view porn. Install the software on all devices you are likely to use.

Two software products worth considering are:

- https://www.covenanteyes.com/
- https://everaccountable.com/pure-desire/

There are many more if you search for them.

Does the software cost much money? Cheaper than a divorce. It will help to solve a difficult problem and make things right with God. You can't put a value on that.

## Cultural Strongholds

Each of us has a worldview, which serves as our personal philosophy about life and defines what is right and wrong. This worldview is shaped by education, friends, upbringing, and our culture. See chapter eight for world views in detail.

This cultural influence and worldview will shape how we view and interpret the Bible. The influence can be positive or negative.

Cultural strongholds in a negative sense are:

- Worldviews that are based on lies
- Philosophies of life that are corrupted by the devil's lies
- A system of lies that has been institutionalized by Satan

All of these will give you a distorted view of scripture and of who God really is. I have seen in many Indian cultures where the God of the Bible is worshipped alongside Brahma and Vishnu. These guys don't have a strong belief in any one God, so they hedge their bets. This is flawed as:

> *You shall not bow down to them or serve them, for I the Lord your God am a jealous God* (Exodus 20:5)

You can't hedge your bets. Either the God of the Bible is God, or He isn't. The process of combining Christianity with traditional beliefs is known as syncretism, and it isn't confined to Indian culture.

The mix of beliefs forms a matrix structure:

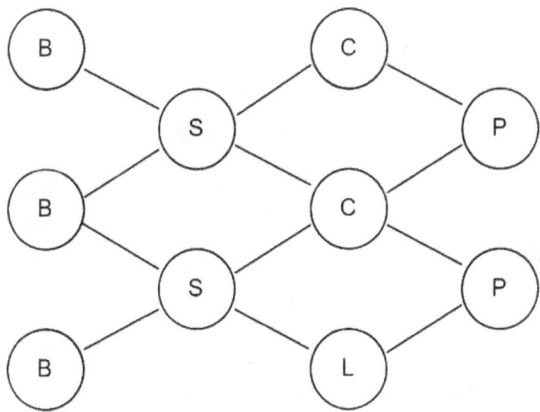

Figure 19.11 – Cultural structure

B is for false belief. S is for Superstition. C for Control. L for Legalism and P for practice. False **B**eliefs lead to **S**uperstitions, leading to **C**ontrol and **L**egalism, which bring forth cultural **P**ractices

The first step to breaking free from this stronghold is to recognise that the stronghold exists in your life. Start by looking at the beliefs held by relatives that give rise to superstitions. Does this lead to legalistic practices? Do these beliefs, superstitions, and practices influence your view of the Bible and who God is? Do you view God as harsh, legalistic, and/or distant? The Bible says God is slow to anger and quick to forgive.

By being aware of the influence of culture while reading and meditating on the Word of God, you will correct any flawed thinking by renewing your mind to the Word of God.

## Religious Strongholds

Religious strongholds can be defined as harmful beliefs or thought patterns that go against God's will. These strongholds can be based on what we know and believe and can shape our actions.

The Pharisees are the best example of this. They were a religious sect that started around 150 BCE, shortly after the Maccabean revolt that freed Israel from Greek rule.[37] The Pharisees were key to re-establishing temple worship. They started off doing the will of God. However, they took the law of Moses and insisted that all believers adopt the priestly purification rituals and then added their own cleansing and purification rituals, turning their faith into a salvation of works, thereby removing the need for grace and mercy from God. After just one hundred and fifty years, they had gone from doing the will of God to opposing the will of God and crucifying Jesus.

In contrast, if we look at the lives of King David and Daniel, these men worshipped and prayed regularly to God. They walked with God and had a relationship with Him. They learned to depend on the grace and mercy of God and not rely on their own capabilities.

So, the nature of a religious stronghold is a legalistic ceremony or ritual that is not described in the Bible and is not required by God. The doctrine will help form the basis of a works-based salvation.

Some organisations will call themselves a church and will mix Biblical doctrine with New Age or occult practices, thereby twisting the truth with a series of lies. The Mormon Church is a classic example, where the founder, Joseph Smith, blended rituals from Freemasonry with Christianity to create a church with distorted doctrines.

This can be a hidden stronghold in that unless you are aware of practices and rituals in your church services that don't align with the Word of God, you may not be aware of the stronghold.

It is also important not to be overly critical. For example, your church chooses to offer communion only once a month. Don't leave your church just because of this. However, if they neglect communion altogether, then that's a problem. In such a case, talk to the pastor. Religious strongholds are often enforced by control. If your pastor has the attitude, "My way or the highway," then it might be time to seek God on where you should be fellowshipping.

The key to breaking free from this stronghold is to seek God for wisdom and guidance. God may want you to stay in that church and help correct the mistakes. If not, He will show you where you should go to be safe and receive sound Bible based doctrine.

## STRONGHOLD OF BITTERNESS

Bitterness has its roots in offence. If you haven't been offended, then you haven't been to church enough. Most people leave a church due to offence. God tests our commitment to Him through the door of offence. Offence, when nurtured by our repetitive thoughts, grows a root of bitterness in our hearts.

My question to you is: "Who has the problem, the offender or the offended?" The offender may not know he or she has offended you. So, you confront them. They tell you that you are off your rocker and to take another happy pill, further offending you. Who then is hurting, you or the perpetrator?

When you are first offended, there is a moment of shock and horror. "I can't believe they said that". You need to mentally process what just happened. This is normal and necessary. However, beyond the initial mental processing, if you continue to play the event over and over in your mind, this will grow a root of bitterness in your heart. The longer you let this weed grow, the more it will hurt you and the harder it will be to up root.

To be free from this stronghold, you have to forgive the offender and then ask God to forgive you for harbouring the resentment. Ask the Holy Spirit to descend on you and heal your innermost parts. This type of prayer time might need to be repeated several times depending on the magnitude of the offence, but it will set you free.

## Stronghold of Jealousy

Jealousy is another weed that grows in your garden and needs to be plucked out while it is small. The longer it is left, and the more you feed it, the greater the strength of this stronghold, making it harder to remove.

Jealousy gives rise to envy, spite, gossip, betrayal, judgment, suspicion, and cruelty. These are not the fruits of the Holy Spirit; rather, they are fruits of sin.

There are essentially two paths to jealousy. It is either derived from a romantic relationship that is under threat or a function of you comparing yourself with someone else. Either way, it will generate feelings of envy, insecurity, resentment, and suspicion.

The root of this stronghold is insecurity driven by low self-esteem. The devil will sow negative thoughts into your mind, using low self-esteem as a foothold. Thoughts like "You're not good enough for Him." "The other guy is so much better looking and comes from a wealthy family. What chance do I have?"

The first step to breaking this stronghold is to recognise and stop these unfounded negative thoughts. If this is a relationship issue, she might not care if you are rich or poor, fat or skinny. Can you read her mind? How accurate are these assumptions?

Do you remember chapter five, where I discussed distortions of the mind? This is a playground for the devil. If you think the other guy has more chances in the relationship than you, then you are assuming, which is a type of mental distortion.

What about non-relationship Jealousy? Have you seen the little rich girl driving the Mercedes down the road? You're thinking she owns the road and the car park because she drives a Mercedes convertible. Stop and do a quick inventory. Are you in Christ? If so, you have inherited eternal life. You have been adopted into God's own family as a child of God, chosen to be a royal priest. Now, about the girl in the car. Is she in Christ? Maybe not.

You can only receive what you are given from God. No good thing will He withhold from those who love Him. If you don't have a Mercedes, that's because it isn't in your best interest.

To smash open this stronghold, recognise that the root is based on unfounded lies that have taken hold due to poor self-esteem and insecurity. Then, ask God to forgive you and release you from this bondage.

Next, you need to stop entertaining those thoughts that feed this stronghold.

Lastly, use the exercise in this chapter under "Structure of Low Self Esteem" to eliminate the foothold that the devil exploited in the first place.

## STRONGHOLD OF CONFUSION

This stronghold can be influenced by demonic forces working internally (demonic oppression) or externally through orchestrated events that the devil has put in place. It can also be purely a mental issue without any spiritual implications.

Mental issues leading to confusion:

- Reconciling conflicting beliefs or ideas
- Information overload
- Ambiguity or lack of understanding of an issue
- Emotional state. Stressed, anxious, or fatigued.
- Lack of prior knowledge [38]

It actually doesn't matter which issue is leading to your state of confusion; your freedom is not far away.

To smash this stronghold open, we need to find the peace of God that passes all understanding. Find a quiet place and open your Bible to Psalm 91. Spend just ten minutes meditating on this Psalm.

> *"He who dwells in the secret place of the Most High Shall abide under the shadow of the Almighty"* (Ps 91:1)

He is your hiding place, your refuge and strength. Ever-present help in times of trouble. In His presence is perfect peace.

Now ask God for clarity of mind and understanding to fill your heart and mind. Let the peace of God fill your heart and mind in Christ Jesus.

## STRONGHOLD OF WORKS

This stronghold forms when work or ministry is used to boost self-worth and self-esteem. The result is that your primary focus becomes your work or ministry. As you become busy, God takes second place, and there is little focus, if any, on spending time with him. This stronghold forms the workaholic and ultimately leads to burnout. Burnout leads to relationship and mental breakdown. It is justified by the need to earn a living or further the kingdom of God. However, in the long term, neither of those objectives can be fulfilled, as neither the church nor corporate organisations can tolerate mental breaks and aggressive outbursts.

Once Satan has this mechanism set up, he can step back and doesn't need to do anything, as you are left to self-destruct. If you attempt recovery, then suddenly a new challenge or more work comes your way to ensure you do not break free from burnout.

The key to breaking this stronghold is to establish boundaries. In everything, there is a time. A time to work, a time to play, a time for family, and a time for God. A sustainable lifestyle will have a balance of all these aspects of life. There is also a priority chain. God first, then family, followed by work and ministry. God needs to be number one in your heart, on a list of one. When work or ministry takes first place, all else will fail.

Ask God for strength and wisdom, to know when to say "No, enough is enough."

## Final Comments

If you are suffering from any stronghold of addiction, whether it be drugs, alcohol, or pornography, then it is very likely that your predominant thought pattern is the next fix, the next drink, or the obsession with the office girl. This makes it an idol that is being exalted above God. God needs to be number one on a list of one.

If there is a stronghold active in your life, your situation is not sustainable. Either you will acknowledge the problem and seek help and be restored to Christ, or you will not consider that you have a problem and keep feeding the stronghold. As you do, over time, you will lose interest in God and the things of God.

Small deviation in the way, over time, leads to large deviation in the way.[4]

# The Church

There is no such thing as a perfect church. If the pastor drives a Mercedes, he's obviously taking home the bingo money. "No one talks to me in that church, they're a bunch of snobs". "The leaders are all stuck up and vain". "There are scumbags in that church". "If I hear one more preach on tithing, I will explode".

Let me start with giving. If you give to the church, you are, in fact, giving to God. What the church then does with that money is none of our business. Hopefully, they send the money to where it can do the most good. The pastor receives a salary, just like you and I; only he is on call 24/7. It's likely he never sees the bingo money, as most churches have an officer who manages the money. If a pastor wants to buy a Mercedes with his salary, what is that to you and I?

Do you remember in chapter five, the section on Distortions of the Mind? It talked about "All or Nothing" thinking. So, when you say, "No one talks to me," how true is that? Are the members snobby? Have you made an effort to connect with anyone?

# THE CHURCH

Every church has its scumbags. These are carnal Christians who talk the talk but don't walk the walk. They are carnal in nature and have failed to die to self. Failed to pick up their cross and follow Jesus. In some churches, these types of people make up the majority of the congregation. On the other hand, every church has great people who would die for what they believe. These are the people to connect with, befriend, and serve Christ with.

*The quality of a man is not found in the number of his possessions but in his (or her) dedication to the things he (or she) believes.* If your view of the church, is that you only see the scumbags, then you are seeing the church through a distortion called filtering. Filtering out the good and acknowledging the bad.

In many churches, you will find that individuals have been promoted to leadership positions before they are adequately prepared for such roles. God does this to develop those leaders and teach them to trust Him. Meanwhile, people like you and me are willing to serve, and our willingness and submission are tested by having to work under someone who is either immature in faith or simply immature.

So, you see, the church is perfect in its imperfection.

> *So now, through the church, the multifaceted wisdom of God in all its countless aspects might now be made known to the rulers and authorities.* (Eph 3:10)

Hopefully, the church you go to preaches the gospel, has worship music that makes it easy to enter into the presence of God, and is making an attempt to reach out to the community. It is so important to go where God wants to plant you and that you prosper in that place.

## Attack on the Church

As a Christian, you will experience attacks from the enemy in two dimensions: internal conflict and external conflict. Just as in individual life, so it is in church life; the church faces both internal and external conflicts.

External conflict usually manifests as an attack from the world, bad publicity, social media rants, or attacks from the local government and council.

Internal conflicts aren't always obvious. They involve members of the church who call themselves followers of Christ. A great deal of the New Testament is dedicated to such people.

## Carnal Believers

We are all carnal to some degree. Born again out of the world, we start off very worldly, and over time, the Lord works on our character to be more like Him. The process is known as sanctification, which begins with dying to self. In chapter five, I talked about having an outward focus and being "Out of the Box". Out of the box, your spiritual eyes are open. This is the first step towards dying to self and living for Christ.

A believer who has failed to die to self and is carnal in mind is only a problem to himself or herself until he or she starts to influence others in the church. This can take the form of gossip, malice, envy, or jealousy. They desire a position of authority as a leader or teacher. Some become self-appointed teachers or prophets. They are the first to gossip and backbite the leadership. Satan will use these people to the detriment of the church, usually to cause division.

## The Enemy Within Believers

Sometimes people from an occult background come to church and give their life to Jesus, but they have either had the demon cast out with the access left open, or the demon has never left in the first place. Either way, this individual unknowingly becomes a plant for the devil—an agent of evil in the house of God. A worse scenario is if the demon-oppressed individual starts manifesting spiritual gifts. These are passed off as gifts of the Holy Spirit, but are not.

## Division

This is by far the greatest problem facing the church today. Satan has successfully divided Catholics from Protestants, Anglicans from Pentecostals, and pastors against pastors. Last I knew, we all believed in the Bible and followed Jesus. Same God, right?

This particular attack is multi-dimensional. It affects the church on a global level, individual denominations, the churches within each denomination, and extends to individual congregations' members.

I have found these different types of divisions within the church:

- Doctrinal – different interpretations of scripture
- Denominational – differences in governance & traditions
- Theological – differences in emphasis of teaching
- Liturgical – differences in style of worship
- Cultural and Ethnic – division based on race or nationality
- Leadership and Authority – division based on authority structure
- Moral and Social – issues relating to moral standards
- Personal and Relational – personal conflict between believers

- Schisms and Heresies – Breakaway groups that form their own movement.

Satan will use all of these avenues at different times to disable the army of God. This is Satan's plan for the church:

> *Every kingdom divided against itself is brought to desolation, and every city or house divided against itself will not stand.* (Matt 12:25)

Thankfully, God has other plans for his church. We all need to follow Paul's instructions:

> *I beseech you to walk worthy of the calling with which you were called, with all lowliness and gentleness, with longsuffering,* **bearing with one another in love**. (Eph 4:1)

## False Teaching

Many of Paul's letters to the churches deal with false teachers who twist doctrine, misinterpret scripture, and do not represent the word of God. Most of the time, this develops from taking scripture out of context. By reading the previous verses and the next few verses of scripture, you gain the context of what is being said. Does the teaching fit the context?

Now, look beyond the words. What is the spirit of the man communicating this message? Is there a spirit of pride? Is the message too legalistic? I don't mean a call to repentance that brings people closer to Christ. I'm referring to the type of legalism the Pharisees used on Jesus's disciples when they complained they weren't washing their hands. This type of legalism focuses on trivial matters and ignores the weightier issues. The Bible tells us:

*Test all things; hold fast what is good* (1 Thes 5:21)

There is a reverse paradigm, where a legitimate teacher teaches without referring to the Bible. Is this wrong? Not necessarily. It is very reasonable to use worldly events and facts to draw illustrations that support Biblical principles. Hold fast to what is good.

## False Prophecy

Prophecy can be fantastic to edify the church.

> *I wish you all spoke with tongues, but even more that you prophesied; for he who prophesies is greater than he who speaks with tongues.* (1 Cor 14:5)

It can also be problematic, as false prophets are at work in the church.

> *Beware of false prophets, who come to you in sheep's clothing, but inwardly they are ravenous wolves.* (Matt 7:15)

The second greatest problem facing the church today is a lack of discernment, and Satan knows this and exploits the situation. In chapter thirteen, I discussed spiritual discernment, where the Holy Spirit convicts you in your spirit when things aren't right. In the absence of such knowledge, you rely on mental discernment. Does the prophecy align with the word of God? Does it correspond with what you already know?

I've seen three types of prophets:

1. Those who prophecy with accuracy
2. Those who prophecy what God tells them and then add their own stuff. Not really knowing where God stopped, and they started.

These are usually loan rangers, not accountable to anyone, so their gift never matures.
3. Those who Prophecy in their flesh and do not hear from God.

There is a danger when the church follows prophecy, knowledge, and revelation from prophets and treats this knowledge as equal to the Word of God. The word given should align with the word of God, and be warned when it doesn't.

God never contradicts His word. If in doubt, shelve the prophecy rather than throw the baby out with the bath water.

## Offence & Unforgiveness

Have you never been offended in church? If not, chances are you haven't been going long enough. I've seen more people leave the church through offence than for any other issue. An offence can disqualify you from attending church.

For four years, I helped with new Christian classes. It was something I was passionate about, and it gave me a lot of pleasure to see people being established.

One day, without warning, I received a text message on my phone: "Thanks for all your help, but you are no longer required to assist with new Christian classes. " It's safe to say I was a tad angry. No, angry isn't cutting it. I was furious. How insensitive. They couldn't even be bothered to phone me. Were they too scared to speak to me face to face? Does my existence in the church mean so little to the management? With this offence, I almost left the church. There were just two options in front of me: leave the church or forgive the individual with poor communication protocols.

I chose to forgive. Leaving a church should only be when God has some other place for you.

Nurturing unforgiveness leads to bitterness and misery. Forgiving an offence is in your best interest.

## Tithing

Tithing, that is, giving a tenth of your income to the church, is widely taught in many churches, and I do understand the need. The more money the church has, the more it can do. You have only two resources to give to God: time and money. However, tithing is an Old Testament teaching and is tied to the Old Covenant. Under the new covenant:

> Each one must give as he has decided in his heart, not reluctantly or under compulsion, for **God loves a cheerful giver.** *(2 Cor 9:7)*

You should, therefore, give what you can afford, not what you can't afford. If you have enough money to feed your family or pay the church, but not both, then prioritise feeding your family. On the other hand, if you are living in abundance, then don't stop at ten percent.

# Spiritual Protection

Revelation chapter two describes seven letters to seven churches. Each letter is a report card from Jesus outlining how they are doing. To the churches of Laodicea and Sardis, Jesus has nothing good to say. These churches are prospering without any persecution or affliction from the enemy. Do you find the same in your life? If so, you need to ask why.

He has nothing bad to say about the churches of Smyrna and Philadelphia. These churches were under the worst persecution. Jesus's response is "You're doing a great job, just hang in there". This chapter is designed to help you hang in there.

In this chapter, I will cover three aspects of protection: the Armour of God, Psalm 91, and warfare prayers of protection. Don't rely on just one aspect for defence; instead, let all your defences come into play.

# Protection 101

# The Whole Armour of God

During the first century AD, the city of Ephesus was the third-largest in the Roman Empire. It held major trade routes to the rest of Asia and was also home to the goddess Hellenic Artemis. Her temple was said to be one of the seven wonders of the world.[39] In addition to this pagan worship, Ephesus was heavily entrenched in witchcraft, occultism, and magic, creating a spiritual stronghold over the people of Ephesus.

Paul, in this letter to the Ephesians, gives the Ephesians instruction on how to protect themselves spiritually.

> *Therefore, take up the whole armour of God, that you may be able to withstand in the evil day, and having done all, to stand. Stand therefore, having girded your waist with truth, having put on the breastplate of righteousness, and having shod your feet with the preparation of the gospel of peace; above all, taking the shield of faith with which you will be able to quench all the fiery darts of the wicked one. And take the helmet of salvation, and the sword of the Spirit, which is the word of God.* (Eph 6:13-17)

At the time of writing this, Paul is under house arrest, chained to a Roman soldier. He becomes well acquainted with the armour of the soldier and sees what that armour might look like from a spiritual point of view. It's interesting how often Paul uses the word "Stand" in this passage. "Withstand in the evil day", "Having done all Stand", and "Stand therefore". The military view here is a stance of a soldier in combat standing firm against the oncoming enemy, and not giving up ground. This is what we are called to do.

Let's break down the elements of the armour in detail.

## *Belt of Truth*

The Roman belt resembled an apron more than a typical belt. Its purpose was to protect the loins and provide strength to the core. A soldier's loins were always a point of vulnerability. At the same time, he needed core strength to wield a sword in one hand and a large shield in the other.

Figure 21.1 – Roman Belt

As believers, we are not just to have truth as part of our character but actively walk in truth. We have to gird our waists with God's truth, which will, in turn, become a part of us. This enables us to be reliable and faithful as God is reliable and faithful.

## Breastplate of Righteousness

The breastplate, known as the thoraka, was a metal plate that covered a leather garment and protected a soldier's vital parts, most importantly, the heart.

Figure 21.2 – Roman Breastplate

Doing what's right protects us by eliminating footholds for the enemy. Have you ever been pulled over for speeding? Perhaps I'm the only one. But if I were doing what's right and adhering to the speed limit, then there are no grounds for a speeding ticket. Could the money lost on a speeding ticket not have been used more wisely?

## Sandals of Peace

Roman soldiers wore a heavy sandal called a caliga. It was a kind of half boot, half sandal which was tied to the leg with leather thonging. The sole was three-quarters of an inch thick, layered leather held together with hobnails, which provided both durability and traction.

Figure 21.3 – Roman Sandal

> *And the peace of God, which surpasses all understanding, will guard your hearts and your minds in Christ Jesus.* (Phil 4:7)

The peace of God, when you have it, is absolutely wonderful. You have peace no matter what your circumstances are around you. You act and respond rationally. Your emotions don't dictate your actions. However, that peace can be taken in a moment of time.

The moment someone sins against you, your initial response is most likely anger and/or disappointment. At that point, your peace has been taken, and you have become the victim, often without cause. You have a right to be angry; you have been hurt unjustifiably. As you mentally process what just happened, you start replaying the event over and over, and this impacts your heart. A root of bitterness begins to grow, and then the devil steps in since you've created a foothold for him to ensure you keep thinking about the event and continue feeding that anger and bitterness.

It's time to ask some hard questions. Do I want to stay angry? Do I want the peace of God back? Can I bring myself to forgive this person? Only in forgiveness are you truly free. This is one of the greatest weapons in spiritual warfare. The truth is, you may not be ready to forgive. That's okay. Just stop feeding the root of bitterness so that when you are ready to forgive, bitterness does not consume you.

I need to stress the need to guard your heart and mind. If the offence is part of a recurring pattern, then that pattern needs to be broken before you can truly forgive. If the perpetrator doesn't think they've done anything wrong, they will need to be confronted to ensure there is no recurrence. Finally, if your situation is physically or psychologically toxic, you may need to remove yourself from the situation completely.

Another scenario is when you overreact to something someone has said. It might not be obvious at first, but you may find a repeating pattern where someone just happens to say something that brings anger to the surface, and that anger quickly turns to rage, and your emotions are out of context with your reality. In these situations, it is likely that whatever was said brought back emotions from a previous hurt. Perhaps even an event you can no longer remember. One defence mechanism the mind uses is to block memories of horrific events. If something happens or something is said that brings these suppressed memories to the surface, then all the emotions connected with that trauma will also surface and be vented.

The first step to solving overreacting is to be aware that it is a problem and then look for the triggers. You may even need some professional counselling to be free from your past trauma. If you really want the peace of God, then seek inner healing.

If you have a button that, when pressed, produces an overreaction, then there will always be someone who presses that button just for entertainment. The devil will make sure of it.

## *Shield of Faith*

The Roman shield was four feet tall and two and a half feet wide, called a scutum. It was made of wood, overlaid with canvas and then leather. A metal rim around the edges held it together.

The darts or arrows that the Romans had to defend against were called plumbata. This short metal weapon was thrown from a distance. These plumbata were often set alight for greater impact. The Roman soldiers would immerse their shields in water, thereby soaking the leather and underlying canvas, so the flaming darts would be extinguished.

Figure 21.4 – Roman shield

# SPIRITUAL PROTECTION

When the Romans were under attack, they raised their shields above their heads. When they did this in unity and locked their shields together, it formed an impenetrable roof.[40]

For most of my Christian life, I thought of the shield of faith in terms of the fiery darts being thoughts planted in my mind by the devil. However, the shield of faith also protects against events sent by the enemy to trouble us and get us off course. The shield of faith is also about taking authority over the works of the enemy.

There are three ways fiery darts can manifest:

1. Thoughts planted by the enemy
2. Words spoken over you by someone
3. Events orchestrated by the enemy.

This equates to attacks of thought, word, and deed.

The key to the shield of faith lies in believing by faith that God will deliver you.

> *No temptation has overtaken you except such as is common to man; but God is faithful, who will not allow you to be tempted beyond what you are able, but with the temptation will also make the way of escape, that you may be able to bear it.* (1 Cor 10:13)

Here are some Scriptures you can pray through for faith:

> *It is for freedom that Christ has set us free. Stand firm then and do not let yourselves be burdened again by a yoke of slavery.* (Gal 5:1)

*Submit yourselves then to God. Resist the devil and he will flee from you.* (James 4:7)

*You are my hiding place; you will protect me from trouble and surround me with songs of deliverance.* (Ps 32:7)

*I sought the Lord, and he answered me; he delivered me from all my fears.* (Ps 34:4)

*The righteous cry out and the Lord hears them; he delivers them from all their troubles.* (Ps 34:17)

## *Helmet of Salvation*

The helmet the Romans wore was mostly bronze and covered the back of the neck and cheeks of the face. Therefore, protecting the head completely.

Figure 21.5 – Roman Helmet

For a long time, I could not join the dots between the Helmet and Salvation. It wasn't until I understood that salvation is so much more than just eternal life, although I was happy with the concept of not going to Sheol for eternity.

> *He predestined and lovingly planned for us to be adopted to Himself as His own children through Jesus Christ* (Eph 1:5)

Adopted? By whom? God. What God? God Most High. Do you mean the God who put two trillion galaxies in the universe just to amaze us when we look up into the sky? Yes, that God. We are to be His own children. Is there anyone higher or greater than God Himself whom we could be adopted by? Is there any greater honour than to be a child of the Most High God?

> *In Him we have redemption that is, our deliverance and salvation through His blood which paid the penalty for our sins and resulted in the forgiveness and complete pardon of our sins.* (Eph 1:7)

Redemption, deliverance, and salvation are gifts to those who accept Jesus as their Lord and Savior. We receive complete pardon for all our wrongdoings. What compares to the promise we have in Him?

> *In Him also we have received an inheritance, having been predestined (chosen before the beginning of time) according to His purposes.* (Eph 1:11)

Predestined? Predestined means we were planned and considered in advance. The advance of what? Before the beginning of time. So, time had a beginning, and we were well-considered ahead of this event. How awesome is our God?

Inheritance? As children of God, we have an inheritance. Who in the known universe has more wealth, more knowledge, more wisdom than the God we serve? How will he who didn't spare His son not give us all things?

> *Even when we were dead by shortcomings and trespasses, He made us alive together in fellowship and in union with Christ* (Eph 2:5)

In fellowship with Christ? This gives us a hint as to where we can expect to spend eternity and with whom. So, where is Christ, with whom I'll be spending so much time?

> *He raised Him from the dead and seated Him at His right hand in the heavenly places Far above all rule and authority and power and dominion and every name not only in this age but the age to come.* (Eph 1:20)

If Jesus is seated at the right hand of the Father and we are seated in fellowship and union with Christ, then we are also seated above all rule, authority, power, and dominion.

We have an inheritance that's beyond belief. In it, there is no more suffering, there is no more striving just to live, and there is no more sickness. The blessing of salvation is nothing short of astonishing.

To prepare for battle, you need to put on the helmet of salvation daily. You do this by meditating on the book of Ephesians, particularly the verses mentioned above.

SPIRITUAL PROTECTION

## *Sword of the Spirit*

The gladius was a double-edged sword 20 to 24 inches long. Mainly used for close combat. The sword is a weapon for advancing and taking ground in battle.[41]

Figure 21.6 – Roman Sword

This is the only offensive weapon mentioned in the passage. The sword of the Spirit is the word of God. Paul implies that we are to engage the enemy with the spoken word of God.

When Jesus was tempted by Satan in the wilderness, he had been without food for forty days and was hungry. Satan's attack is recorded in Matt 4:3. He said: "If you are the Son of God, command that these stones become bread." Jesus replies in Matt 4:4, "It is written, man shall not live by bread alone, but by every word that proceeds from the mouth of God."

Jesus was actually quoting Deut 8:3:

> *So He humbled you, allowed you to hunger, and fed you with manna which you did not know nor did your fathers know, that He might make you know that man shall not live*

*by bread alone; but man lives by every word that proceeds from the mouth of the Lord* (Deut 8:3)

In Matthew 4:4, we see an example of speaking the Word of God and declaring it against the enemy. The spoken Word of God is the instrument of the Spirit that we, as believers, need to proclaim against the schemes of the devil to break his strongholds and declare freedom.

## Protection 102
## Psalm 91

An effective protection of yourself and your loved ones can come from meditating on Psalm 91.

> *He who dwells in the secret place of the Most High Shall abide under the shadow of the Almighty. I will say of the Lord, "He is my refuge and my fortress; My God, in Him I will trust."* (Ps 91:1)

*He who dwells in the **secret place**.* The secret place is that intimate place where you meet with God and worship Him. It's within you. In that place, there is perfect peace, understanding, and the love of the Father. In that place, you can revive your spirit and rise up on wings like eagles. You can run and not grow weary.

*He who **dwells** in the secret place shall abide under the shadow of the Almighty.* The condition to abide under the shadow of the Almighty is to dwell in the secret place. This does not mean reading your Bible and praying 24/7, but rather meditating on the word and praying often enough that your soul is filled with the mind of Christ and the peace of God.

# SPIRITUAL PROTECTION

> *Surely, He shall deliver you from the snare of the fowler And from the perilous pestilence. He shall cover you with His feathers, And under His wings, you shall take refuge; His truth shall be your shield and buckler.* (Ps 91:3)

*Surely, He shall **deliver you** from the snare of the fowler.* A fowler is someone who catches and kills birds. They set snares that are camouflaged, making them invisible to the bird. The poor bird doesn't see it coming. So if you are dwelling in the secret place of the Most High, he promises to protect you from these invisible snares and from the fowler who wants to take your life.

"*Under **His wings**, you shall take refuge.*" Who's wings? Wings bring to mind the imagery of a large bird, such as an eagle. *Under His Wings* brings imagery of a chick under the wings of a large bird, where it is safe and secure. "His wings" aren't referring to a bird. They refer to the Most High God. No one is more powerful or greater. How safe are you if you are under His wing? This is a good segue into the next verse.

> *You shall not be afraid of the terror by night, Nor of the arrow that flies by day, Nor of the pestilence that walks in darkness, Nor of the destruction that lays waste at noonday.* (Ps 91:5)

"*You shall not be afraid of the **terror** by night.*" This is the terror you don't see coming. You are not aware of the pending danger. "*Nor of the **arrow** that flies by day.*" These are afflictions you see coming but are powerless to avoid.

"*Nor of the **pestilence** that walks in darkness.*" This is a deadly pestilence. Things that can take your life. It walks in darkness. You don't see it coming.

"Nor the **destruction** that **lays waste** at noonday." Devastation that happens in plain sight.

> *A thousand may fall at your side, And ten thousand at your right hand, but it shall not come near you. Only with your eyes shall you look, And see the reward of the wicked.* (Ps 91:7)

"A thousand may fall at your side, And ten thousand at your right hand, but it **shall not come near you**." A thousand on one side and ten thousand on the other side. The exact numbers aren't important, other than to say, a multitude of people, all around you. Sickness may be all around, *but it shall not come near you.* Flu may be infecting everyone around you, *but it shall not come near you.* People may be retrenched all around you, *but it shall not come near you.*

> *Because you have made the Lord, who is my refuge, Even the Most High, your dwelling place, No evil shall befall you, Nor shall any plague come near your dwelling* (Ps 91: 9)

"Because you have made the lord who is my refuge, even the Most High, your dwelling." Because you chose to dwell in the secret place of the Most High, all these blessings of protection against known and unknown issues exist for YOU.

## PROTECTION 103

### PRAYERS OF PROTECTION

The answer to how to pray for protection over yourself and your family lies in knowing the schemes of the enemy and praying against them, particularly by identifying and destroying traps set by the enemy. The prayers that follow are an extract from a book called "Fire Prayers" by John Ramirez. His book contains the greatest collection of pinpoint prayers for protecting your loved ones and breaking demonic forces. You will likely need this book as a reference, as I do.

## *Prayers to drive Demons out of your Home*

By the fire of the Holy Spirit, I completely purify my home in Jesus' name. I reclaim my home from the forces of darkness and the devil, and I dedicate it once again to Jesus Christ. Amen.

I dedicate my family to Jesus Christ. I commit the foundations of our home to Him. I dedicate every room in this house to Jesus Christ. Holy Spirit, you are welcome in this place. Please purify and sanctify my home, my marriage, my children, their rooms, their clothing, every closet, and the attic. In the name of Jesus, Amen.

## *Prayers of Protection for Marriages*

In the name of Jesus, I command every demonic force and spirit that attempts to frustrate my marriage to be destroyed. In Jesus' name, I also rebuke all demonic discord and division that is attacking my marriage. Amen.

In Jesus' name, I break the spirits of poverty, perversion, alcohol, and every demonic weakness that seeks to imprison my marriage. Amen.

## *Prayers of Protection for Your Children*

I break off from my child(ren) all brainwashing, all satanic entrapment, and every false identity of homosexuality, perversion, or pornography, in Jesus' name.

I break every satanic scheme that keeps my child(ren) addicted to electronic devices, including tablets and cell phones. I destroy all mechanisms that have manipulated or brainwashed them by infiltrating their minds, souls, and thinking. Let it all drown in the blood of Jesus. Amen.

## *Prayers of Protection from Sickness*

I command every evil sickness and every infirmity spirit that has been planted in my body by the devil to leave my body now, in the name of Jesus. (Name each sickness. Lay your hands on your head or wherever the sickness is. Then, with the anointing and fire of the Holy Spirit, command that devil to come out, in the name of Jesus.)

By the fire of the Holy Spirit, I ask the Holy Spirit to purify and sanctify my body from all demonic pollution and every demonic sickness and infirmity that has gripped my body, in Jesus' name.

## *Prayers of Protection of Finance*

In Jesus' name, I nullify every plot, scheme, and device of the enemy that is meant to cause financial failure in my life.

In Jesus' name, I break every demonic curse or manipulation that has caused me to spend money unnecessarily and lose all my potential to create wealth.

## *Prayers to Break Demonic Control*

In the name of Jesus, I break, destroy, and uproot any legal ground that I have given to any demon, whether known or unknown.

I sever all generational curses of rebellion, witchcraft, lust, poverty, pride, idolatry, egotism, death, premature death, destruction, sickness, infirmity, and fear. I renounce every mind-control spirit. I release myself from all rejection and self-rejection now, in the name of Jesus. [42]

# Intercession

Prayer is defined as an act of communication between humans and God almighty. Communication is the fundamental building block of relationships. God wants us to be in a relationship with Him, and that can only be achieved with communication through prayer.

So, what kind of communication do you think God wants to hear? Do you approach Him like a child with a list of requests? Give me, give me, give me. There will be times when this is appropriate and necessary.

When you sit down to pray:

1. Start by praising Him for who He is. The God that created everything, including you. The God who loves you more than your mother ever did. The God who is all-knowing, all-powerful, and all-loving. To Him who sits on the throne and unto the Lamb.
2. Thank Him for what He's done. Are you still breathing? That's a good outcome. Are you living in the knowledge of Christ? That

means you are free from condemnation and have eternal life in paradise. Should we not be thankful?
3. Thank Him for what He's doing. Are you in good health? Is your family safe? Do you have a steady job? Perhaps things aren't going so well, and that's why you are petitioning the Almighty for help. In faith, start thanking Him for the solution.
4. Appeal to His nature. He is a loving and merciful God. Rich in mercy and grace, because of his deep, wonderful, and intense love with which he loves us. Now bring your petitions to him with thanksgiving.

> *Be anxious for nothing, but in everything by prayer and supplication, with thanksgiving, let your requests be made known to God.* (Phil 4:6)

After a period of worship and thanksgiving, you can bring your requests and petitions to Him. At this point, you are interceding. This is what is known as intercessory prayer. It is always wise to ask God how you should pray for a situation. If you are addressing demonic strongholds, you will need to begin with a strategy from God.

There are three pillars of prayer:

- Faith
- Perseverance
- Specifics

## Faith

> *But without faith it is impossible to please him: for he that cometh to God must believe that he is, and that he is a rewarder of them that diligently seek him* (Heb 11:6)

Faith is the key to activating the power of God. Faith comes from hearing, and hearing comes from the rhema word of God. The word rhema refers to the spoken or personally applied Word of God. This is often the revelation you receive from meditating on the Word of God. As you meditate on the Word of God, it changes your heart to be more like Christ. The key revelation you need to understand is Eph 1:19:

> *And [so that you will begin to know] what the immeasurable and unlimited and surpassing greatness of His [active, spiritual] power is in us who believe.* (Eph 1:19)

Once you understand in your heart that the power that raised Christ from the dead is active and alive within you, you will be UNSTOPPABLE.

Let's look at another example of faith in action. Matt 15:22-29

> *A Canaanite woman from that vicinity came to him, crying out, "Lord, Son of David, have mercy on me! My daughter is demon-possessed and suffering terribly." Jesus did not answer a word. So his disciples came to him and urged him, "Send her away, for she keeps crying out after us." He answered, "I was sent only to the lost sheep of Israel." The woman came and knelt before him. "Lord, help me!" she said. He replied, "It is not right to take the children's bread and toss it to the dogs." "Yes it is, Lord," she said. "Even the dogs eat the crumbs that fall*

*from their master's table." Then Jesus said to her, "Woman, you have great faith! Your request is granted." And her daughter was healed at that moment.* (Matt15:22-29)

This is only the second scripture in the Bible where someone is commended for great faith. Notice both her persistence and her humility. Jesus refers to her as a dog unworthy of the children's bread. Instead of taking offence, she humbles herself. 'Yes Lord, even the dogs are worthy of the crumbs that fall from the master's table" (Paraphrased). Do you see how Jesus tests her faith? Will you let offence get in the way of what you truly seek?

> *The heartfelt and persistent prayer of a righteous man (believer) can accomplish much [when put into action and made effective by God—it is dynamic and can have tremendous power].* (James 5:16)

## Persistence

God does not always answer prayers immediately. Sometimes, you need to persevere until you achieve a breakthrough. Let's read what Jesus has to say regarding perseverance in Luke 18:1-8.

> *Then Jesus told his disciples a parable to show them that they should always pray and not give up. He said: "In a certain town there was a judge who neither feared God nor cared what people thought. And there was a widow in that town who kept coming to him with the plea, 'Grant me justice against my adversary.'*

> "For some time he refused. But finally, he said to himself, 'Even though I don't fear God or care what people think, yet because this widow keeps bothering me, I will see that she gets justice, so that she won't eventually come and attack me!'"
>
> And the Lord said, "Listen to what the unjust judge says. And will not God bring about justice for his chosen ones, who cry out to him day and night? Will he keep putting them off? I tell you, he will see that they get justice, and quickly. However, when the Son of Man comes, will he find faith on the earth?"

There are times when you are praying for the breaking of strongholds from someone. These strongholds could be drugs, lust, negative thinking, or spiritual blindness brought on by demonic oppression. They may be spiritual or mental in nature, but either way, your prayers will weaken the stronghold, and at some point, the victim will break free.

There is also a type of prayer called travailing, which can take long periods of time. In the case of travailing, you are birthing something in the spirit. It is this type of intercessory prayer that leads to miraculous healing.

> And let us not grow weary while doing good, for in due season we shall reap if we do not lose heart. (Gal 6:9)

## SPECIFIC

The more we know about an issue or person, the more specific we can pray. God is into specifics, pinpointed, targeted prayer. For example, if you are praying for the cancer diagnosis of a loved one to be cured. Cursing the word cancer is a very general prayer. Breaking off a spirit of infirmity is helpful only if a spirit of infirmity is responsible for the cancer. How you pray for a person with cancer depends on whether they can believe in supernatural healing or whether they will seek medical help.

If they are not seeking medical help, then you need to stand with them in faith. The specifics you need to pray for are around keeping negative, unbelieving people away and surrounding them with the angels of God to encourage them. Keep them strong and positive, and their faith will be built up by the Word of God. Remember that a cancer cell is a malformed cell, irrespective of the type of cancer. If God can create the Heavens and the Earth out of nothing, is it too difficult for Him to change a malformed cell into a healthy cell? Can he not then heal even cancer in an instant?

If they are seeking medical help, then it helps to know the type of cancer and how it might be treated. Will the doctors use chemotherapy, radiation therapy, or both? What stage is the cancer? Stage four cancer is often too advanced to treat. Supernatural faith is needed. A stage one cancer may not need an operation. The key thing you might pray for is Godly wisdom for the doctors. They will make the right diagnosis. The treatment will be effective, without complications, allowing the tumour to shrink and be removed with ease, ensuring that no secondaries will be found elsewhere in the body.

Be mindful that as situations and circumstances change, your approach to prayer may also need to change. For instance, if secondary cancers are detected elsewhere in the body, this indicates that the cancer has spread, prompting doctors to alter their approach to the situation.

I have used cancer here as an example, but the same principle of understanding specifics and praying through those specifics applies to many different areas.

> *The heartfelt and persistent prayer of a righteous man (believer) can accomplish much [when put into action and*

*made effective by God—it is dynamic and can have tremendous power]*. (James 5:16)

## FASTING

Fasting with prayer is like a turbocharger for a car. It has the power to smash the enemies' strongholds. However, it must be applied with a good deal of common sense.

Fasting is the act of abstaining from something for a period of time for a spiritual purpose. This usually involves food and sometimes fluids. However, it can also refer to abstaining from television, social media, or coffee. The point is to refrain from something you frequently do or consume.

There are many different types of Fasting, but they boil down to these three:

- Partial Fast
- Full fast (Liquid only)
- Absolute fast (No food or Liquid)

### *Partial Fast*

If you are fasting from food, then this could be considered a Daniel fast, where you abstain from meat and alcohol. If you are fasting from television or social media, then you could restrict yourself to thirty minutes a day.

### *Full fast*

In a full fast, you stop all food for a period of time. Liquids are acceptable and are encouraged around mealtime. Your body clock will trigger hunger pains around the time you expect your meal. This is an excellent opportunity to drink some fluids and seek God. Water and fruit juice are good liquid options. Avoid milk, as it stimulates the digestive system and may lead to increased hunger pains. When hunger pains arise, focus your spirit and mind on worship instead of the pain and discomfort. You will find that within an hour, the pain and discomfort will subside. If the discomfort does not subside or the pain becomes acute, then stop the fast and, if necessary, seek professional health advice.

## *Absolute Fast*

In an absolute fast, you are abstaining from both food and liquids. It is possible to go forty days without food; however, after more than three days without liquid, your organs begin to shut down. The damage can be permanent or fatal. Only proceed with this type of fast if you are sure the Lord is leading you to, and even then, only with medical supervision. Three days is the maximum duration for this type of fast.

## *How Long Do You Fast?*

If you are new to fasting, then start with a short fast of one meal, either lunch or dinner. If a single meal fast is successful, then try fasting for two meals, lunch and dinner. This results in a twenty-four-hour fast. Longer fasts are possible with the right start and end approaches. If you begin with a long fast and fail, then you are likely not to try fasting again.

I personally limit my full fasting to three days, starting on a Friday and carrying the fast over the weekend. In this way, my fasting has zero impact on my work life. Your situation may be different.

## *Start Fasting*

If you are fasting for more than one day, ensure your last two meals before the fast are small and rich in fruits or vegetables. This way, your stomach will begin to shrink prior to the fast, resulting in fewer digestive juices when there is no food present.

## *End Fasting*

The end of a fast is nearly the opposite of a start. Your first meal should be small and consist of fruits or vegetables that are easy to digest. The first meal should exclude red meat. Introduce some fish or chicken in the second meal, increasing the portion slightly. By the third meal, you should return to normal.

Please don't make the same mistake I keep making. Most times, after a period of successful prayer and fasting, I treat myself to a nice meal. That in itself is not so bad. But I then tend to eat more than is typical for me, which has the effect of expanding the stomach beyond where it was prior to the fast. A smart play is not to overeat after a fast but to keep your portions small. In that way, you will continue to lose weight.

**Tips**:
- Get plenty of rest
- Do some exercise and get fresh air. Walk and pray.
- Consume plenty of fluids (Pure bottled water)
- Be on guard for spiritual attack from the enemy

## FINAL COMMENTS

If you have health complications like diabetes, you should not fast. If you are fasting and you suddenly get chest pains or shortness of breath, then stop fasting. If chest pain persists, then seek medical help. [43]

# Intercession That Backfires

If you read enough spiritual warfare books, you can come away believing you have all the power and authority to take on the devil at any level. "I'm gona go get'em." The words "any level" may not be absolutely true.

> Therefore take up the whole armour of God, that you may be able to withstand in the evil day, and having done all, to **stand**. (Eph 6:13)

The word "stand" seems to stand out. After putting on the full armour of God, we don't pull out the bazooka and blow them to pieces. Why does Paul tell us to stand and not charge?

## Encouragement to Charge

While writing this book, I attended a Christian conference, and a young Māori man got up to speak on Spiritual Warfare. He was very enthusiastic about the subject and could perform the Māori Haka (Māori war dance). He proceeded to teach about the ANZAC tradition and a little-known battle in which Australian and New Zealand troops had run out of food and bullets, having nothing but bayonets. Armed only with bayonets, they charged an army equipped with machine guns, preferring to die in battle than live.

Encouragement empowers us to act. But there is a point of being too enthusiastic where we act without wisdom.

After reading Peter Wagner's book, "Breaking Spiritual Strongholds in Your City", [44] I was inspired by all the victories mentioned, detailing how they took city after city for Christ. There was very little mention of the spiritual attacks faced while overcoming demonic strongholds. I believe the success of these spiritual warfare initiatives was due to the leaders consistently seeking God for guidance at every step, seeking wisdom every step of the way.

## Why Not Charge

In his book "Needless Casualties of War", John Paul Jackson outlines numerous instances of people who had miscarriages, developed cancer, or died suddenly. All on the back of having tried to bind demonic forces over geographical areas (territorial spirits). [45]

I remember a passionate youth pastor in my old church who had a lovely wife and two kids. Sometime after he left the church, I met him in a video shop (yes, there used to be shops where you could rent videos to watch at home). The section where he was picking movies from was dedicated to pornography. He had lost his ministry and his family.

We are not engaged in a short-term battle. The battle will more than likely last as long as you remain on the earth. Whatever ministry or ministries you are involved in must be sustainable in the long term. The youth pastor mentioned above had placed ministry first, God second, and family last. This hierarchical order is neither sustainable nor biblically correct.

## **WRESTLING LEVIATHAN**

The Bible talks about wrestling with a sea monster called Leviathan, which can be compared to fighting a territorial spirit. Let's look at Job chapter forty-one.

> *"Can you draw out Leviathan with a hook, Or snare his tongue with a line which you lower? Can you put a reed through his nose, or pierce his jaw with a hook? Will he make many supplications to you? Will he speak softly to you? Will he make a covenant with you? Will you take him as a servant forever? Will you play with him as with a bird, or will you leash him for your maidens? Will your companions make a banquet of him? Will they apportion him among the merchants? Can you fill his skin with harpoons, Or his head with fishing spears? Lay your hand on him; Remember the battle— Never do it again!* (Job 41:1-8)

Then, there is a further description of the creature.

> *Who can open the doors of his face, With his terrible teeth all around? His rows of scales are his pride, Shut up tightly as with a seal; One is so near another That no air can come*

> between them; They are joined one to another, They stick together and cannot be parted. His sneezings flash forth light, And his eyes are like the eyelids of the morning. Out of his mouth go burning lights; Sparks of fire shoot out. Smoke goes out of his nostrils, As from a boiling pot and burning rushes. His breath kindles coals, And a flame goes out of his mouth. (Job 41:14-21)

The Leviathan is a very fierce sea creature. If you are taking on territorial spirits, they are likely a type of Leviathan. They are fierce, strong, well-armed, and can eat you for breakfast.

Isaiah Identifies the Leviathan with the Serpent and Satan.

> In that day the LORD with His severe sword, great and strong, Will punish Leviathan the fleeing serpent, Leviathan that twisted serpent; And He will slay the reptile that is in the sea. (Isaiah 27:1)

Notice it's the Lord that punishes Leviathan and not the prophet.

## TAKING ON TERRITORIAL SPIRITS

You might recall that in chapter fifteen, I mentioned that unclean spirits were the foot soldiers for Satan and that fallen angels took up positions of authority as territorial spirits. We don't usually have authority over territorial spirits. The story that follows reveals the consequences of making such an assault.

The Northern Beaches of Sydney, where I live, have one of the highest rates of youth suicide in the country. Two of my fellow church members, Clair and Tracy, decided they would team up (two or more in agreement) to bind the demonic force and lose the captives. Suddenly, Clair began experiencing severe migraines, and Tracy barely slept at night. This went on for several months. They sought prayer and healing everywhere they could. They had taken on Leviathan and were not under any church covering.

*Remember the battle— Never do it again*

About a year later, the Holy Spirit spoke to Tracy about starting a fortnightly prayer meeting that would involve the entire church. Clair and Tracy had the right idea, but they were out of step with God's timing and God's plan.

## FINAL COMMENTS

My Māori friend, who had enthusiastically tried to inspire warriors for the battle, was only inspiring for a short-term battle, which would leave its casualties.

Never deal with Territorial Strongholds alone. Understand that the enemy's plan will try to separate and isolate you from others. Unity is always key to seeing sustainable victory in a region.

We need to follow God's lead in spiritual warfare and not get ahead of the Holy Spirit.

> *Then Jesus answered and said to them, "Most assuredly, I say to you, the Son can do nothing of Himself, but what He sees the Father do; for whatever He does, the Son also does in like manner.* (John 5:19)

Jesus only did what He saw His Father doing. We need to follow His example and be guided in any initiative of warfare. Therefore, if it is on your heart to take on a Territorial Spirit, begin by seeking God for a strategy. You might remember from chapter fifteen how Satan petitions God to gain access to us. Thus, we can petition God on how to best bring down spiritual strongholds. This will almost certainly involve one or two others.

The strategy that God gives you may be as simple as meeting once a week to pray. It may involve walking down the streets where you live at night, praying over each house. Whatever God shows you, do that in obedience and then wait for further instructions. It is important to partner with God and not get ahead of Him or lag behind. By partnering with God, your success is guaranteed.

# Evicting Demonic Squatters

Our enemy will stop at nothing to ensure you never reach your full potential in Christ. The more Christ-like you become, the more of a threat you are to the devil's plans.

Four reasons Christians may be unaware of demonic activity:

1. Fear of demons causes people to deny their existence.
2. Lack of spiritual discernment
3. Most modern preaching and teaching avoid the subject of demonic activity.
4. First-century faith has largely been replaced by twentieth-century rationalism. We cannot rationalize spiritual matters with our minds alone.

Demons can inhabit individuals, objects, areas of land, or entire territories, depending on their purpose. They can gain access through sin, trauma, victimisation, witchcraft, occult practices, or curses.

Possible symptoms of a spiritually polluted atmosphere:

- Sudden chronic illness
- Recurrent bad dreams and nightmares
- Insomnia
- Behavioural problems
- Relational problems (Continual fighting and arguing)
- Lack of Peace
- Restless, disturbed children
- Unexplained illness or bondage to sin
- Ghosts or demonic apparitions
- Poltergeists
- Foul, unexplainable odours
- Atmospheric heaviness, making it hard to breathe
- Continual nausea and headaches

If you are experiencing any of these things on an ongoing basis, ask the lord to reveal any spiritual darkness that may be in your home.

## When Demons Inhabit Objects

Demons can attach themselves to various objects. Many of these objects unknowingly enter our homes. Types of problematic objects include:

- Foreign Gods – These are typically idols purchased from overseas holidays. On the surface, they appear harmless. However, our God is a jealous God, and having idols in your home creates multiple problems, not just opening a door to the devil.
- False Religions – items or literature regarding other religions. This also includes Yoga, Transcendental meditation, mantras, and texts of Eastern mysticism.

- Occult Objects – this includes tarot cards, crystals, and anything that can be associated with the occult.
- Secret Society Objects – Secret societies will guide you through some kind of initiation ceremony. The ceremony will involve objects that have demonic attachments.

Chapter two of this book briefly covers my journey into martial arts and occultism. To break free, I had to get rid of all my books. The books I knew were of an occult nature, I burnt them, and the rest I dumped in the garbage bin. The ashes of the burnt books filled one garbage bin, while the books I didn't burn filled three garbage bins. One book, in particular, was personally signed by the Grand Master of Togakure Ryu himself, and it meant a great deal to me. However, there comes a time when you need to put your feelings aside and do what's necessary. Had I not destroyed the books, I would have been spiritually held back at best and not following Christ today, at worst.

In chapter three, I had two friends who brought me gifts. I had been a Christian for several years at that point, so my house and life were spiritually clean. My girlfriend at the time (now my wife) sensed a heaviness in the atmosphere, which she directly attributed to a warrior shield and bow set from New Guinea. We removed these gifts and took authority over the demonic squatters, evicting them in the name of Jesus. We then prayed to fully sanctify the house, declaring it to be a house of God for His purposes. We asked the Holy Spirit to fill every room with His divine presence.

The demonic squatters were evicted that day.

## When Demons Inhabit Land and Property

Demonic forces can take up residence on land and any dwelling on that land. This is usually due to either past demonic activities or a door opened through sin. Whatever the source may be, these unwelcome guests need to go.

When my wife and I bought our first home together, by chance, we found out the previous occupants were a young married couple who had divorced. Now, God didn't explicitly speak to either of us about demonic strongholds in the house. But rather than assume it was spiritually clean, we made an assumption it wasn't spiritually clean and that the conflict between the two previous occupants may have opened the door to the demonic realm.

With this in mind, we went room by room, binding the spirit of divorce, the spirit of depression, and the spirit of strife. We then asked for the Holy Spirit to come and fill each room afresh. Our spiritual attack was not limited to the house, but we went into the yard and to the boundary of the property, casting out any demonic influence that may have taken up residence. Were we being super spiro? Possibly. But if so, no harm done. If, on the other hand, we were right and the property needed cleansing, then such an action would save us much grief.

## Steps to Evicting Demonic Squatters

The following is a guide to evicting demonic squatters. This is best done with someone else who can pray with you and take authority with you, ideally, a spouse or close friend whom you not only trust but also know is strong in the Lord.

1. Remove all demonic objects and literature

Go through your home, room by room, and ask the Lord to show you what must go. This is not always obvious. When you find a book or artifact purchased in Asia, it is not sufficient to simply sell it at a garage sale or throw it in the garbage. Occult books must be burned. Religious artifacts must be destroyed. If you sell them, you are passing the problem to someone else and profiting from it transaction.

2. Take your authority and evict those demonic forces

    On a room-by-room basis, claim your authority as a child of the Most High God. By the authority of Jesus Christ, command all demonic forces, religious spirits, and spirits of evil to leave and never return. Remind them that "You are a defeated foe." "Your days are numbered." "You no longer have any foothold in my house." "You are simply NOT welcome."

3. Invite the Holy Spirit to fill your home and your life

    Pray this prayer: "I invite the presence of the Holy Spirit to fill this house. Father, I dedicate this house as a house of God. I ask that you come down and fill it completely with your divine presence. That any visitor who comes to the door will know and experience the tangible presence of you."

4. Stay Vigilant

    Stay vigilant and watch for changes in the atmosphere that may indicate the enemy gaining access again. The enemy may flee for a time, but he will be eager to take up residency, if possible. The playing of worship music is an effective way to maintain a Godly atmosphere and deter demonic squatters from taking up residence.

# Epilogue

There are many other books for could read on spiritual warfare, by many great authors. But there is only one you really need to read, and that is the Bible. Everything you actually need is in that book.

## The Bible

The Bible could be summed up as the history of salvation. The first few verses introduce the problem. Man's fall due to Satan's temptation in the garden of Eden. From that point the story builds and there are numerous stories of heroes for God. The story climaxes with the four gospels and Jesus arriving on earth. His crucifixion is the high point of the entire book. The epistles that follow the gospels could be viewed as an anti-climax to the story with the book of Revelation bringing the story to an end. But it's not an end, it's a new beginning. A new Heaven and a new Earth, with a new Jerusalem made of transparent gold. You know the ending, YOU WIN.

## Highly Structured

As you dig deeper into the Bible, you will find it is highly structured beyond what our modern computers can produce. One example of this is the Torah code. Equal distance lettering, which is found in the first five books of the Bible, appears only in Hebrew. Theologians found by taking letters at equal distances apart from within the text that the letters formed words or names, that are nearly impossible to have happened by chance. Around Genesis chapter thirty-seven, theologians found a chronological list of names: Boaz, Obed, Jesse, and David. The text was written some four hundred years before any of these people walked the Earth. The only conclusion you can come to from this is that the author was from outside of time.[46]

## HIGHLY MYSTICAL

The book is a highly mystical book, filled with knowledge that's beyond knowing. You can capture it in your heart, but you can't capture it in your head. A finite being cannot fathom an infinite God.

The power of God is found in the Word of God. It is by meditating on the Word of God that you are transformed from the inside out. As you reflect on how the word or passage relates to you, it travels from your head to your heart. You begin to be filled with the spirit of God. You put on the mind of Christ, and you become the hands and feet of Christ himself.

While writing this book, I began meditating on the book of Ephesians. It took me two weeks to reach the end of verse six. How did I get there so quickly? I cheated; I started at verse three.

Let's see how this played out.

*Blessed by the God and Father of our Lord Jesus Christ*
(Eph 1:3)

# EPILOGUE

Blessed by the God and Father of YOUR Lord Jesus Christ. Few people on the planet can call Jesus Lord. If you can call him Lord, then you are one of the few, and you are blessed.

> *Who has blessed us in Christ with every spiritual blessing in heavenly places (Eph 1:3)*

He has blessed YOU with every spiritual blessing in heavenly places? What kind of blessings are spiritual? They are those that don't perish or break; the types that are not temporal but permanent. I cannot begin to fathom or articulate what every spiritual blessing could be, but I know it exceeds what my tiny mind can conceive. Where are these blessings? In heavenly places, where no moth can eat them and no thief can steal them.

> *He chose us in Him before the foundation of the world* (Eph 1:4)

He chose us. He chose YOU. You might think you chose Christ as your saviour, but He chose you. You have been chosen out of a world of sinners, not because you were a good boy or girl, but by the grace of God. The grace He extended to you in love.

> *That we should be holy and without blame before Him in Love.* (Eph 1:4)

There are days when I don't feel very holy. I don't feel blameless. I, and probably you, have all fallen short of the glory of God. But in Christ, he sees us as holy and blameless, even when we are not.

> *Having predestined us to adoption as sons by Jesus Christ to Himself* (Eph 1:5)

Predestined, planned, and purposed for YOU to be adopted. Into whose family are you adopted? Himself, God Almighty. The God who created the universe. Can you grasp the magnitude of the statement? You are saved by grace from destruction. That's wonderful. You will live forever. But God did not plan for you to be an illegitimate child. He planned to adopt you as a son or daughter. Is it honouring enough just to be a servant in the house of God? As a son or daughter, you have an inheritance; you will have a place of your own. You have honour and authority as a son or daughter of the King of the universe. I can no longer find words to articulate this further. The blessing is more than my tiny mind can conceive.

Is it any wonder the Bible says we are more than conquerors through Christ, who loves us? The key to your spiritual survival is remaining in Christ. The key to remaining in Christ is the Word of God on the inside.

# Notes

[1] Buzan, Tony. 2009. *The Memory Book*. Pearson Education Ltd
[2] Rabi R. Maharaj, 1984, Death of a Guru. Hodder Faith
[3] Wilson & Weldon. 1980. Occult Shock and Psychic Forces. Master Books
[4] Miyamoto Musashi. 1645. The Book of Five Rings
[5] Henry Cloud. 1998. The Mom Factor. Zondervan
[6] Christopher Foster. 2023. Killing Selfishness..Advantage Inspirational
[7] Institute, Arbinger. 2002. Leadership and Self Deception. Berrett-Koehler
[8] McKay & Fanning. 2000. Self Esteem. New Harbinger Publications
[9] Scott Alan. 2025. Rejection Rehab. Scott Allan Publishing
[10] Roman Crucifixion Methods Reveal the History of Crucifixion. https://www.biblicalarchaeology.org/daily/biblical-topics/crucifixion/roman-crucifixion-methods-reveal-the-history-of-crucifixion/
[11] Phil Pringle. 2003. Who we are, what we have. PAX Ministries
[12] James Sire.2020.The Universe Next Door
[13] Deism.https://en.wikipedia.org/wiki/Deism
[14] https://plato.stanford.edu/search/searcher.py?query=Naturalism
[15] https://en.wikipedia.org/wiki/Nihilism
[16] Postmodernism.https://www.tate.org.uk/art/art-terms/p/postmodernism
[17] Britannica.https://www.britannica.com/topic/postmodernism-philosophy
[18] Prophet Muhammad.632.The Qur'an
[19] Nithila. 2024. Exploring the Psychological Impact of Movies on Society https://www.linkedin.com/pulse/exploring-psychological-impact-movies-society-the-mind-and-company-vegic/
[20] Video Games and Mental Health. https://www.charliehealth.com/post/video-games-and-mental-health
[21] Albert Mehrabian.1972. Silent Messages. Wadsworth Publishing

22. Robinson, Lawrence. 2024. Social Media and Mental Health. https://www.helpguide.org/articles/mental-health/social-media-and-mental-health.htm
23. Edward T Welch. 2023. When People are Big and God is small. New Growth Press
24. What is Peer Pressure? Examples and Ways to Cope.. https://www.unishanoi.org/about/calendar-news-and-publications/post-default/~board/news/post/what-is-peer-pressure-in-teenagers-and-how-to-handle-it
25. Different Types of Peer Pressure Examples and Coping Strategies. 2023. https://mentalhealthcenterkids.com/blogs/articles/types-of-peer-pressure
26. Peer Pressure. https://psychology.iresearchnet.com/school-psychology/peer-relationships/peer-pressure/?utm_source=chatgpt.com#google_vignette
27. Callin O'Connor and James Owen Weatherall. 2019. The Misinformation Age. Yale University Press
28. The Psychology of Conspiracy Theories. https://pmc.ncbi.nlm.nih.gov/articles/PMC5724570/
29. The Cultural Context for the Hair. https://theologyintheraw.com/the-cultural-context-for-the-hair-length-style-vs-head-coverings-debate-in-1-cor-11-the-meaning-of-kephale-part-12/
30. James W Goll. 2006. Dream Language. Destiny Image Publishers
31. Adam F Thompson. 2009. The Divinity Code: The Keys to Decoding Your Dreams and Visions. Destiny Image
32. Dr Henry Cloud 2017. Boundaries. HarperCollins
33. War in Heaven & Earth Part 1.2023. https://www.youtube.com/watch?v=MvkxXvu-Xys
34. Dr. Ed Murphy.1992.The Handbook for Spiritual Warfare. Thomas Nelson
35. Transactional Analysis in Psychotherapy. 1961.Eric Berne. Mockingbird Press
36. Judith S Beck.2020. Cognitive Behavior Therapy: Basics and Beyond. The Guilford Press
37. Pharisees. https://www.worldhistory.org/Pharisees/
38. Mental Health Magazine. 2024. https://www.psychologs.com/the-psychology-behind-confusion/?srsltid=AfmBOor3LKw261NXpVTcauj2BWMLgkyRJRhRlljgOEQULmp1lrNQ2MjQ
39. Navigating an Ancient Faith. https://navigatinganancientfaith.com/explore/biblical-ephesus
40 Testudo formation. https://en.wikipedia.org/wiki/Testudo_formation
41 The Roman Gladius. https://warfarehistorynetwork.com/article/the-roman-gladius
42 John Ramirez. 2023. Fire Prayers. Charisma House
43 Derek Prince. 1976. How to Fasting successfully. Whitaker House

## NOTES

[44] Peter C Wagner. 2015. Breaking Spiritual Strongholds in your City. Destiny Image Publications
[45] John Paul Jackson. 2009. Needless Casualties of War. Streams Publishing
[46] Treasures in the Family Trees. https://www.khouse.org/personal_update/articles/2004/treasures-family-trees

# About the Author

Roger Robins is a devoted husband and father of two daughters, both actively serving the Lord. A long-time member of large Pentecostal Church in Sydney, Australia, Roger has served in a range of ministries over the past 30+ years, including intercessory prayer, new Christian foundations, and outreach.

His background in martial arts and his personal experiences with the spiritual realm give him a unique perspective on spiritual warfare. With over 40 years of walking with Christ, Roger brings hard-won wisdom, biblical insight, and real-life experience to this powerful guide.

www.ingramcontent.com/pod-product-compliance
Lightning Source LLC
Chambersburg PA
CBHW060500090426
42735CB00011B/2049